Eastward Hoe by Ben Jonson, George Chapman & John Marston

As It was playd in the Black-friers.

By The Children of her Maiesties Reuels.

I0142849

Benjamin "Ben" Jonson was born in June, 1572. A contemporary of William Shakespeare, he is best known for his satirical plays; Volpone, The Alchemist, and Bartholomew Fair, and his equally accomplished lyric poems.

A man of vast reading and a seemingly insatiable appetite for controversy, including time in jail and a penchant for switching faiths, Jonson had an unparalleled breadth of influence on Jacobean and Caroline playwrights and poets.

In 1616 Jonson was appointed by King James I to receive a yearly pension of £60 to become what is recognised as the first official Poet Laureate.

He died on the 6th of August, 1637 at Westminster and is buried in the north aisle of the nave at Westminster Abbey.

A master of both playwriting and poetry his reputation continues to endure and reach a new audience with each succeeding generation.

Index of Contents

DRAMATIS PERSONAE

TOUCHSTONE	A goldsmith.
QUICKSILVER	}
GOLDING	} His apprentices.
SIR PETRONEL FLASH.	
SECURITY	An old usurer.
BRAMBLE	A lawyer.
SEAGULL	A sea captain.
SCAPETHRIFT	}
SPENDALL	} Adventurers bound for Virginia.
SLITGUT	A butcher's apprentice.
POLDAVY	A tailor.
HOLDFAST	}
WOLF	} Officers of the Counter.
HAMLET	A footman.
POTKIN	A tankard-bearer.
TOBY	A prisoner.
MISTRESS TOUCHSTONE.	
GERTRUDE	}
MILDRED	} Her daughters.
WINIFRED	Wife to Security.
SINDEFY	Mistress to Quicksilver.
BETTRICE	A waiting woman.
MISTRESS FOND.	
MISTRESS GAZER.	

Drawer, Coachman, Scrivener, Page, Constable, Officers, Messenger, Two Prisoners and their Friend, Gentlemen.

THE SCENE — LONDON AND THAMES-SIDE

PROLOGUS

Not out of envy, for there's no effect
Where there's no cause; nor out of imitation,
For we have evermore been imitated;
Nor out of our contention to do better
Than that which is oppos'd to ours in title,

For that was good; and better cannot be:
And, for the title, if it seem affected,
We might as well have call'd it, "God you good even:"
Only that eastward westwards still exceeds —
Honor the sun's fair rising, not his setting.
Nor is our title utterly enforc'd,
As by the points we touch at you shall see.
Bear with our willing pains, if dull or witty;
We only dedicate it to the City.

ACT I — SCENE I

Enter MASTER TOUCHSTONE and QUICKSILVER at several doors, QUICKSILVER with his hat, pumps, short sword and dagger, and a racket trussed up under his cloak. At the middle door, enter GOLDING, discovering a goldsmith's shop and walking short turns before it.

TOUCHSTONE - And whither with you now? what loose action are you bound for? Come, what comrades are you to meet withal? where's the supper? where's the rendezvous?

QUICKSILVER - Indeed, and in very good sober truth, sir—

TOUCHSTONE - "Indeed, and in very good sober truth, sir!" Behind my back thou wilt swear faster than a French footboy, and talk more bawdily than a common midwife; and now "indeed, and in very good sober truth, sir!" But, if a privy search should be made, with what furniture are you rigg'd now? Sirrah, I tell thee, I am thy master, William Touchstone, goldsmith; and thou my prentice, Francis Quicksilver; and I will see whither you are running. Work upon that now!

QUICKSILVER - Why, sir, I hope a man may use his recreation with his master's profit.

TOUCHSTONE - Prentices' recreations are seldom with their masters' profit. Work upon that now! You shall give up your cloak, though you be no alderman. — (TOUCHSTONE uncloaks QUICKSILVER.) Heyday! Ruffians Hall! Sword, pumps, here's a racket indeed!

QUICKSILVER - Work upon that now!

TOUCHSTONE - Thou shameless varlet! dost thou jest at thy lawful master, contrary to thy indentures?

QUICKSILVER - Why, 'zblood, sir! my mother's a gentlewoman, and my father a justice of peace and of quorum; and, though I am a younger brother and a prentice, yet I hope I am my father's son; and by God's lid, 't is for your worship and for your commodity that I keep company. I am entertain'd among gallants, true; they call me cousin Frank, right; I lend them moneys, good; they spend it, well. But, when they are spent, must not they strive to get more? Must not their land fly? — and to whom? Shall not your Worship ha' the refusal? Well, I am a good member of the City, if I were well considered. How would merchants thrive, if gentlemen would not be unthrifts? How could gentlemen be unthrifts if their humors were not fed? How should their humors be fed but by whitemeat and cunning secondings? Well, the City might consider us. I am going to an ordinary now: the gallants fall to play; I carry light gold with me. The gallants call, "Cousin Frank, some gold for silver;" I change, gain by it; the gallants lose the gold, and then call, "Cousin Frank, lend me some silver." Why—

TOUCHSTONE - Why? I cannot tell. Seven score pound art thou out in the cash; but look to it, I will not be gallanted out of my moneys. And, as for my rising by other men's fall, God shield me! Did I gain my wealth by ordinaries? no! by exchanging of gold? no! by keeping of gallants' company? no! I hired me a little shop, fought low, took small gain, kept no debt book, garnished my shop, for want of plate, with good wholesome thrifty sentences: as, "Touchstone, keep thy shop, and thy shop will keep thee;" "Light gains makes heavy purses;" "'T is good to be merry and wise." And, when I was wiv'd, having something to stick to, I had the horn of suretyship ever before my eyes. — [to the audience] You all know the device of the horn, where the young fellow slips in at the butt end, and comes squeez'd out at the buccal. — And I grew up, and, I praise Providence, I bear my brows now as high as the best of my neighbors: but thou — well, look to the accounts; your father's bond lies for you: seven score pound is yet in the rear.

QUICKSILVER - Why, 'slid, sir, I have as good, as proper gallants' words for it as any are in London — gentlemen of good phrase, perfect language, passingly behav'd; gallants that wear socks and clean linen, and call me "kind cousin Frank," "good cousin Frank," for they know my father: and, by God's lid, shall not I trust 'em? — not trust?

Enter a PAGE, as inquiring for Touchstone's shop.

GOLDING - What do ye lack, sir? what is 't you'll buy, sir?

TOUCHSTONE - Ay, marry sir; there's a youth of another piece. There's thy fellow-prentice, as good a gentleman born as thou art: nay, and better mean'd. But does he pump it, or racket it? Well, if he thrive not, if he outlast not a hundred such crackling bavins as thou art, God and men neglect industry.

GOLDING - (to the Page) It is his shop, and here my master walks.

TOUCHSTONE - With me, boy?

PAGE - My master, Sir Petronel Flash, recommends his love to you, and will instantly visit you.

TOUCHSTONE - To make up the match with my eldest daughter, my wife's dilling, whom she longs to call madam. — He shall find me unwillingly ready, boy. (Exit PAGE.) — [to the audience] There's another affliction too. As I have two prentices, the one of a boundless prodigality, the other of a most hopeful industry, so have I only two daughters: the eldest, of a proud ambition and nice wantonness; the other, of a modest humility and comely soberness. The one must be ladyfied, forsooth, and be attir'd just to the court cut and long tail. So far is she ill-natur'd to the place and means of my preferment and fortune that she throws all the contempt and despite hatred itself can cast upon it. Well, a piece of land she has; 't was her grandmother's gift; let her and her Sir Petronel flash out that; but, as for my substance, she that scorns me, as I am a citizen and tradesman, shall never pamper her pride with my industry, shall never use me as men do foxes — keep themselves warm in the skin, and throw the body that bare it to the dunghill. I must go entertain this Sir Petronel. — Golding, my utmost care 's for thee, and only trust in thee; look to the shop. — As for you, Master Quicksilver, think of husks, for thy course is running directly to the prodigal's hogs' trough; husks, sirrah! Work upon that now!

Exit TOUCHSTONE.

QUICKSILVER - Marry faugh, Goodman Flat-cap! 'Sfoot! though I am a prentice, I can give arms; and my father's a justice a' peace by descent, and, 'zblood! —

GOLDING - Fie, how you swear!

QUICKSILVER - 'Sfoot, man, I am a gentleman, and may swear by my pedigree, God's my life! Sirrah Golding, wilt be ruled by a fool? Turn good fellow, turn swaggering gallant, and "let the welkin roar, and Erebus also." Look not westward to the fall of Don Phœbus, but to the east — Eastward Ho!

Where radiant beams of lusty Sol appear,
And bright Eous makes the welkin clear.

We are both gentlemen, and therefore should be no coxcombs; let's be no longer fools to this flat-cap, Touchstone, — Eastward, bully! — this satin belly and canvas-back'd Touchstone. 'S life, man! his father was a malt man, and his mother sold gingerbread in Christ Church.

GOLDING - What would ye ha' me do?

QUICKSILVER - Why, do nothing; be like a gentleman, be idle; the curse of man is labor. Wipe thy bum with testones, and make ducks and drakes with shillings. What, Eastward Ho! Wilt thou cry, "What is 't ye lack?" — stand with a bare pate and a dropping nose, under a wooden penthouse, and art a gentleman? Wilt thou bear tankards, and mayst bear arms? Be rul'd; turn gallant. Eastward Ho! — Ta ly re, ly re ro! "Who calls Jeronimo? Speak, here I am." — Gods-so! how like a sheep thou look'st; a' my conscience, some cowherd begot thee, thou Golding of Golding Hall! Ha, boy?

GOLDING - Go; ye are a prodigal coxcomb! I a cowherd's son, because I turn not a drunken, whore-hunting rakehell like thyself?

QUICKSILVER - Rakehell? rakehell?

Offers to draw, and GOLDING trips up his heels and holds him.

GOLDING - Pish, in soft terms, ye are a cowardly, bragging boy. I'll ha' you whipp'd.

QUICKSILVER - Whipp'd? — that's good, i' faith! Untruss me!

GOLDING - No, thou wilt undo thyself. Alas! I behold thee with pity, not with anger; thou common shot-clog, gull of all companies; methinks I see thee already walking in Moorfields without a cloak, with half a hat, without a band, a doublet with three buttons, without a girdle, a hose with one point, and no garter, with a cudgel under thine arm, borrowing and begging threepence.
Takes his sword, and releases him.

QUICKSILVER - Nay, 'slife! take this and take all. As I am a gentleman born, I'll be drunk, grow valiant, and beat thee.

Exit.

GOLDING - Go, thou most madly vain, whom nothing can recover but that which reclaims atheists, and makes great persons sometimes religious — calamity. As for my place and life, thus I read:
Whate'er some vainer youth may term disgrace,

The gain of honest pains is never base;
From trades, from arts, from valor, honor springs;
These three are founts of gentry, yea, of kings.

Exit.

SCENE II - A ROOM IN TOUCHSTONE'S HOUSE

Enter GERTRUDE, MILDRED, BETTRICE, and POLDAVY a tailor; POLDAVY with a fair gown, Scotch farthingale, and French fall in his arms; GERTRUDE in a French head attire and citizen's gown; MILDRED sewing; and BETTRICE leading a monkey after her.

GERTRUDE - For the passion of patience, look if Sir Petronel approach — that sweet, that fine, that delicate, that — for love's sake, tell me if he come. Oh, sister Mil, though my father be a low-capp'd tradesman, yet I must be a lady; and I praise God my mother must call me Madam. Does he come? — Off with this gown, for shame's sake; off with this gown: let not my knight take me in the city cut in any hand: tear 't, pax on 't! — Does he come? tear 't off. — [singing] "Thus, whilst she sleeps, I sorrow for her sake," etc.

MILDRED - Lord, Sister, with what an immodest impatiency and disgraceful scorn do you put off your city tire. I am sorry to think you imagine to right yourself in wronging that which hath made both you and us.

GERTRUDE - I tell you I cannot endure it; I must be a lady. Do you wear your quoif with a London licket, your stammel petticoat with two guards, the buffin gown with the tuft-taffety cape and the velvet lace. I must be a lady, and I will be a lady. I like some humors of the city dames well: to eat cherries only at an angel a pound, good; to dye rich scarlet black, pretty; to line a grogram gown clean thorough with velvet, tolerable; their pure linen, their smocks of three pounds a smock, are to be borne withal. But your mincing niceries, taffeta pipkins, durance petticoats, and silver bodkins — God's my life, as I shall be a lady, I cannot endure it! — Is he come yet? Lord, what a long knight 't is! — [singing] "And ever she cried, 'Shoot home'!" — And yet I knew one longer— "And ever she cried, 'Shoot home,' fa, la, ly, re, lo, la!"

MILDRED - Well, Sister, those that scorn their nest, oft fly with a sick wing.

GERTRUDE - Bow-bell!

MILDRED - Where titles presume to thrust before fit means to second them, wealth and respect often grow sullen, and will not follow. For sure in this I would for your sake I spake not truth: where ambition of place goes before fitness of birth, contempt and disgrace follow. I heard a scholar once say that Ulysses, when he counterfeited himself mad, yok'd cats and foxes and dogs together to draw his plough, whilst he followed and sowed salt; but, sure, I judge them truly mad, that yoke citizens and courtiers, tradesmen and soldiers, a goldsmith's daughter and a knight. Well, Sister, pray God my father sow not salt too.

GERTRUDE - Alas! poor Mil, when I am a lady, I'll pray for thee yet, i' faith: nay, and I'll vouchsafe to call thee Sister Mil still; for, though thou art not like to be a lady as I am, yet sure thou art a creature of God's making; and mayest peradventure to be sav'd as soon as I. — Does he come? — [singing]

"And ever and anon she doubled in her song." Now, Lady's my comfort! what a profane ape's here! Tailor, Poldavy, prithee, fit it, fit it: is this a right Scot? Does it clip close, and bear up round?

POLDAVY - Fine and stiffly, i' faith; 't will keep your thighs so cool, and make your waist so small; here was a fault in your body, but I have supplied the defect, with the effect of my steel instrument, which, though it have but one eye, can see to rectify the imperfection of the proportion.

GERTRUDE - Most edifying tailor! I protest you tailors are most sanctified members, and make many crooked things go upright. How must I bear my hands? light? light?

POLDAVY - Oh, ay; now you are in the lady-fashion, you must do all things light. Tread light, light. Ay, and fall so; that's the court amble.
She trips about the stage.

GERTRUDE - Has the court ne'er a trot?

POLDAVY - No, but a false gallop, lady.

GERTRUDE - [singing] "And if she will not go to bed—"

BETTRICE – The knight's come, forsooth.

GERTRUDE - Is my knight come? O the Lord, my band! Sister, do my cheeks look well? Give me a little box a' the ear, that I may seem to blush; now, now! So, there, there, there!

Enter SIR PETRONEL, MASTER TOUCHSTONE, and MISTRESS TOUCHSTONE.

Here he is! O my dearest delight! Lord, Lord! and how does my knight?

TOUCHSTONE - Fie! with more modesty.

GERTRUDE - Modesty! Why, I am no citizen now. Modesty? Am I not to be married? Y' are best to keep me modest, now I am to be a lady!

SIR PETRONEL - Boldness is good fashion and court-like.

GERTRUDE - Ay, in a country lady I hope it is, as I shall be. And how chance ye came no sooner, knight?

SIR PETRONEL - Faith, I was so entertain'd in the progress with one Count Epernoum, a Welsh knight; we had a match at balloon, too, with my Lord Whachum, for four crowns.

GERTRUDE - At baboon? Jesu! you and I will play at baboon in the country, knight!

SIR PETRONEL - Oh, sweet lady: 't is a strong play with the arm.

GERTRUDE - With arm or leg, or any other member, if it be a court sport. And when shall 's be married, my knight?

SIR PETRONEL - I come now to consummate it; and your father may call a poor knight son-in-law.

TOUCHSTONE - Sir, ye are come. What is not mine to keep I must not be sorry to forgo. A hundred pound land her grandmother left her; 't is yours. Herself, as her mother's gift, is yours. But, if you expect aught from me, know my hand and mine eyes open together: I do not give blindly. Work upon that now!

SIR PETRONEL - Sir, you mistrust not my means? I am a knight.

TOUCHSTONE - Sir, sir, what I know not, you will give me leave to say I am ignorant of.

MISTRESS TOUCHSTONE - Yes, that he is a knight! I know where he had money to pay the gentlemen ushers and heralds their fees. Ay, that he is a knight! And so might you have been too, if you had been aught else than an ass, as well as some of your neighbors. An I thought you would not ha' been knighted, as I am an honest woman, I would ha' dubb'd you myself. I praise God I have wherewithal. But, as for you, Daughter ——

GERTRUDE - Ay, Mother, I must be a lady tomorrow; and, by your leave, Mother (I speak it not without my duty, but only in the right of my husband), I must take place of you, Mother.

MISTRESS TOUCHSTONE - That you shall, Lady-Daughter, and have a coach as well as I, too.

GERTRUDE - Yes, Mother. But by your leave, Mother (I speak it not without my duty, but only in my husband's right), my coach horses must take the wall of your coach horses.

TOUCHSTONE - Come, come, the day grows low. 'T is supper time: use my house; the wedding solemnity is at my wife's cost; thank me for nothing but my willing blessing; for — I cannot feign — my hopes are faint. And, sir, respect my daughter; she has refus'd for you wealthy and honest matches, known good men, well moneyed, better traded, best reputed.

GERTRUDE - Body a' truth! chitizens, chitizens! Sweet knight, as soon as ever we are married, take me to thy mercy out of this miserable chity; presently carry me out of the scent of Newcastle coal and the hearing of Bow-bell; I beseech thee, down with me, for God sake!

TOUCHSTONE - Well, Daughter, I have read that old wit sings:
The greatest rivers flow from little springs:
Though thou art full, scorn not thy means at first;
He that's most drunk may soonest be athirst.
Work upon that now!

All but TOUCHSTONE, MILDRED, and GOLDING depart.

No, no! yond' stand my hopes. — Mildred, come hither, Daughter. And how approve you your sister's fashion? how do you fancy her choice? what dost thou think?

MILDRED - I hope, as a sister, well.

TOUCHSTONE - Nay, but, nay, but how dost thou like her behavior and humor? Speak freely.

MILDRED - I am loath to speak ill; and yet — I am sorry of this — I cannot speak well.

TOUCHSTONE - Well; very good, as I would wish; a modest answer. — Golding, come hither; hither, Golding. How dost thou like the knight, Sir Flash? Does he not look big? How lik'st thou the elephant? He says he has a castle in the country.

GOLDING - Pray Heaven, the elephant carry not his castle on his back.

TOUCHSTONE - 'Fore Heaven, very well! But, seriously, how dost repute him?

GOLDING - The best I can say of him is, I know him not!

TOUCHSTONE - Ha, Golding! I commend thee, I approve thee, and will make it appear my affection is strong to thee. My wife has her humor, and I will ha' mine. Dost thou see my daughter here? She is not fair, well-favored or so, indifferent, which modest measure of beauty shall not make it thy only work to watch her, nor sufficient mischance to suspect her. Thou art towardly, she is modest; thou art provident, she is careful. She's now mine. Give me thy hand; she's now thine. Work upon that now!

GOLDING - Sir, as your son, I honor you; and, as your servant, obey you.

TOUCHSTONE - Sayest thou so? — Come hither, Mildred. Do you see yond' fellow? He is a gentleman, though my prentice, and has somewhat to take too: a youth of good hope; well friended, well parted. Are you mine? You are his. Work, you, upon that now!

MILDRED - Sir, I am all yours; your body gave me life; your care and love, happiness of life; let your virtue still direct it, for to your wisdom I wholly dispose myself.

TOUCHSTONE - Say'st thou so? Be you two better acquainted. — Lip her, lip her, knave. So, shut up shop; in. We must make holiday.

Exeunt GOLDING and MILDRED.

This match shall on, for I intend to prove
Which thrives the best, the mean or lofty love:
Whether fit wedlock vow'd 'twixt like and like,
Or prouder hopes, which daringly o'erstrike
Their place and means. 'T is honest time's expense,
When seeming lightness bears a moral sense.
Work upon that now.

Exit.

ACT II — SCENE I – GOLDSMITH'S ROW. THE INNER STAGE REPRESENTS TOUCHSTONE'S STALL

TOUCHSTONE, GOLDING, and MILDRED are discovered sitting on either side of the stall.

TOUCHSTONE - Quicksilver! — Master Francis Quicksilver! — Master Quicksilver!

Enter QUICKSILVER.

QUICKSILVER - Here, sir; (ump!)

TOUCHSTONE - So, sir; nothing but flat "Master Quicksilver," without any familiar addition will fetch you. Will you truss my points, sir?

QUICKSILVER - Ay, forsooth; (ump!)

TOUCHSTONE - How now, sir! the drunken hiccup so soon this morning?

QUICKSILVER - 'Tis but the coldness of my stomach, forsooth.

TOUCHSTONE - What! have you the cause natural for it? Y' are a very learned drunkard: I believe I shall miss some of my silver spoons with your learning. The nuptial night will not moisten your throat sufficiently, but the morning likewise must rain her dews into your gluttonous we asand.

QUICKSILVER - An 't please you, sir, we did but drink (ump!) to the coming off of the knightly bridegroom.

TOUCHSTONE - To the coming off an him?

QUICKSILVER - Ay, forsooth, we drunk to his coming on (ump!), when we went to bed; and, now we are up, we must drink to his coming off: for that's the chief honor of a soldier, sir; and therefore we must drink so much the more to it, forsooth (ump!)

TOUCHSTONE - A very capital reason! So that you go to bed late, and rise early to commit drunkenness! You fulfil the scripture very sufficient wickedly, forsooth.

QUICKSILVER - The knight's men, forsooth, be still a' their knees at it (ump!) and because 'tis for your credit, sir, I would be loath to flinch.

TOUCHSTONE - I pray, sir, e'en to 'em again, then; y'are one of the separated crew, one of my wife's faction, and my young lady's, with whom, and with their great match, I will have nothing to do.

QUICKSILVER - So, sir; now I will go keep my (ump!) credit with 'em, an 't please you, sir.

TOUCHSTONE - In any case, sir, lay one cup of sack more a' your cold stomach, I beseech you.

QUICKSILVER - Yes, forsooth.

Exit QUICKSILVER.

TOUCHSTONE - This is for my credit! Servants ever maintain drunkenness in their master's house for their master's credit — a good idle serving man's reason. I thank Time the night is past; I ne'er wak'd to such cost; I think we have stow'd more sorts of flesh in our bellies than ever Noah's ark received; and, for wine, why my house turns giddy with it, and more noise in it than at a conduit. Ay, me, even beasts condemn our gluttony. Well, 'tis our city's fault, which, because we commit seldom, we commit the more sinfully; we lose no time in our sensuality, but we make amends for it. Oh, that we would do so in virtue and religious negligences! But see, here are all the sober parcels my house can show. I'll eavesdrop — hear what thoughts they utter this morning.

GOLDING and MILDRED come forward.

GOLDING - But is it possible that you, seeing your sister preferr'd to the bed of a knight, should contain your affections in the arms of a prentice?

MILDRED - I had rather make up the garment of my affections in some of the same piece than, like a Fool, wear gowns of two colors, or mix sackcloth with satin.

GOLDING - And do the costly garments, the title and fame of a lady, the fashion, observation, and reverence proper to such preferment, no more inflame you than such convenience as my poor means and industry can offer to your virtues?

MILDRED - I have observ'd that the bridle given to those violent flatteries of fortune is seldom recover'd; they bear one headlong in desire from one novelty to another; and where those ranging appetites reign, there is ever more passion than reason: no stay, and so no happiness. These hasty advancements are not natural. Nature hath given us legs to go to our objects; not wings to fly to them.

GOLDING - How dear an object you are to my desires I cannot express; whose fruition would my master's absolute consent and yours vouchsafe me, I should be absolutely happy. And, though it were a grace so far beyond my merit that I should blush with unworthiness to receive it, yet thus far both my love and my means shall assure your requital: you shall want nothing fit for your birth and education; what increase of wealth and advancement the honest and orderly industry and skill of our trade will afford in any, I doubt not will be aspir'd by me; I will ever make your contentment the end of my endeavors; I will love you above all; and only your grief shall be my misery, and your delight my felicity.

TOUCHSTONE - [aside] Work upon that now! By my hopes, he woos honestly and orderly; he shall be anchor of my hopes. Look, see the ill-yok'd monster, his fellow!

Re-enter QUICKSILVER, unlac'd, a towel about his neck, in his flat cap, drunk.

QUICKSILVER - Eastward Ho! "Holla, ye pampered jades of Asia!"

TOUCHSTONE - [aside] Drunk now downright, a' my fidelity!

QUICKSILVER - (Ump!) Pulldo, pulldo! showse, quoth the caliver.

GOLDING - Fie, fellow Quicksilver, what a pickle are you in!

QUICKSILVER - Pickle? Pickle in thy throat; 'zouns, pickle! — Wa, ha, ho! — Good morrow, knight Petronel. — Morrow, lady Goldsmith. — Come off, knight, with a counterbuff, for the honor of knighthood.

GOLDING - Why, how now, sir? Do ye know where you are?

QUICKSILVER - Where I am? Why, 'sblood, you jolt-head, — where I am!

GOLDING - Go to, go to, for shame go to bed, and sleep out this immodesty; thou sham'st both my master and his house.

QUICKSILVER - Shame? what shame? I thought thou wouldst show thy bringing up; an thou wert a gentleman as I am, thou wouldst think it no shame to be drunk. Lend me some money; save my credit; I must dine with the serving men and their wives — and their wives, sirrah!

GOLDING - E'en who you will; I'll not lend thee threepence.

QUICKSILVER - 'Sfoot; lend me some money; "hast thou not Hyren here?"

TOUCHSTONE - Why, how now, sirrah? what vein's this, ha?

QUICKSILVER - "Who cries on murther? Lady, was it you?" How does our master? Pray thee, cry "Eastward Ho!"

TOUCHSTONE - Sirrah, sirrah, y'are past your hiccup now; I see y' are drunk —

QUICKSILVER - 'Tis for your credit, Master.

TOUCHSTONE - And hear you keep a whore in town.

QUICKSILVER - 'Tis for your credit, Master.

TOUCHSTONE - And what you are out in cash I know.

QUICKSILVER - So do I. My father's a gentleman. Work upon that now! Eastward Ho!

TOUCHSTONE - Sir, "Eastward Ho" will make you go Westward Ho! I will no longer dishonest my house, nor endanger my stock with your license. There, sir: there's your indenture; all your apparel (that I must know) is on your back; and from this time my door is shut to you: from me be free; but, for other freedom and the moneys you have wasted, "Eastward Ho" shall not serve you.

QUICKSILVER - Am I free a' my fetters? Rent, fly with a duck in thy mouth; and now I tell thee, Touchstone —

TOUCHSTONE - Good sir—

QUICKSILVER - "When this eternal substance of my soul—"

TOUCHSTONE - Well said; change your gold ends for your play ends.

QUICKSILVER - "Did live imprison'd in my wanton flesh—"

TOUCHSTONE - What then, sir?

QUICKSILVER - "I was a courtier in the Spanish court,
And Don Andrea was my name."

TOUCHSTONE - Good Master Don Andrea, will you march?

QUICKSILVER - Sweet Touchstone, will you lend me two shillings?

TOUCHSTONE - Not a penny.

QUICKSILVER - Not a penny? I have friends, and I have acquaintance; I will piss at thy shop posts, and throw rotten eggs at thy sign. Work upon that now!

Exit, staggering.

TOUCHSTONE - Now, sirrah, you! hear you? You shall serve me no more neither—not an hour longer.

GOLDING - What mean you, sir?

TOUCHSTONE - I mean to give thee thy freedom, and with thy freedom my daughter, and with my daughter a father's love; and, with all these, such a portion as shall make knight Petronel himself envy thee! Y' are both agreed, are ye not?

GOLDING - With all submission, both of thanks and duty.

TOUCHSTONE - Well then, the great power of Heaven bless and confirm you. And, Golding, that my love to thee may not show less than my wife's love to my eldest daughter, thy marriage feast shall equal the knight's and hers.

GOLDING - Let me beseech you, no, sir; the superfluity and cold meat left at their nuptials will, with bounty, furnish ours. The grossest prodigality is superfluous cost of the belly; nor would I wish any invitement of states or friends; only your reverend presence and witness shall sufficiently grace and confirm us.

TOUCHSTONE - Son to mine own bosom, take her and my blessing. The nice fondling, my Lady Sir-reverence, that I must not now presume to call daughter, is so ravish'd with desire to hansel her new coach and see her knight's Eastward Castle, that the next morning will sweat with her busy setting forth. Away will she and her mother; and, while their preparation is making, ourselves, with some two or three other friends, will consummate the humble match we have in God's name concluded.

'Tis to my wish; for I have often read,
Fit birth, fit age, keeps long a quiet bed.
'Tis to my wish; for tradesmen, well 'tis known,
Get with more ease than gentry keeps his own.

Exeunt.

SCENE II – BEFORE SECURITY'S HOUSE

Enter SECURITY, solus.

SECURITY - My privy guest, lusty Quicksilver, has drunk too deep of the bride-bowl; but, with a little sleep, he is much recovered; and, I think, is making himself ready to be drunk in a gallanter likeness. My house is as 't were the cave where the young outlaw hoards the stolen vails of his occupation; and here, when he will revel it in his prodigal similitude, he retires to his trunks, and (I may say softly) his punks: he dares trust me with the keeping of both; for I am security itself; my name is Security, the famous usurer.

Enter QUICKSILVER in his prentice's coat and cap, his gallant breeches and stockings, gartering himself.

QUICKSILVER - Come, old Security, thou father of destruction! th' indented sheepskin is burn'd wherein I was wrapp'd; and I am now loose, to get more children of perdition into thy usurous bonds. Thou feed'st my lechery, and I thy covetousness; thou art pander to me for my wench, and I to thee for thy cozenages. K. me, K. thee runs through court and country.

SECURITY - Well said, my subtle Quicksilver! These K's ope the doors to all this world's felicity; the dullest forehead sees it. Let not Master Courtier think he carries all the knavery on his shoulders: I have known poor Hob in the country, that has worn hobnails on 's shoes, have as much villainy in 's head as he that wears gold buttons in 's cap.

QUICKSILVER - Why, man, 't is the London highway to thrift; if virtue be us'd, 't is but as a scrap to the net of villainy. They that use it simply, thrive simply, I warrant. Weight and fashion makes goldsmiths cuckolds.

Enter SINDEFY, with QUICKSILVER'S doublet, cloak, rapier, and dagger.

SINDEFY - Here, sir, put off the other half of your prenticeship.

QUICKSILVER - Well said, sweet SINDEFY - Bring forth my bravery.
Now let my trunks shoot forth their silks conceal'd;
I now am free, and now will justify
My trunks and punks. Avaunt, dull flat cap, then!
Via, the curtain that shadowed Borgia!
There lie, thou husk of my envassall'd state;
I, Samson, now have burst the Philistines' bands,
And in thy lap, my lovely Dalila,
I'll lie and snore out my enfranchis'd state.

[Singing]

When Samson was a tall young man,
His power and strength increased than;
He sold no more nor cup nor can;
But did them all despise.
Old Touchstone, now write to thy friends
For one to sell thy base gold ends;
Quicksilver now no more attends
Thee, Touchstone.

But, dad, hast thou seen my running gelding dress'd to-day?

SECURITY - That I have, Frank. The ostler a' th' Cock dressed him for a breakfast.

QUICKSILVER - What, did he eat him?

SECURITY - No, but he ate his breakfast for dressing him; and so dress'd him for breakfast.

QUICKSILVER - O witty age! where age is young in wit,
And all youths' words have graybeards full of it!

SINDEFY - But alas, Frank! how will all this be maintain'd now? Your place maintain'd it before.

QUICKSILVER - Why, and I maintain'd my place. I'll to the court: another manner of place for maintenance, I hope, than the silly city. I heard my father say, I heard my mother sing an old song and a true: "Thou art a she fool, and know'st not what belongs to our male wisdom." I shall be a merchant, forsooth! trust my estate in a wooden trough as he does? What are these ships but tennis balls for the winds to play withal? — toss'd from one wave to another; now under-line, now over the house; sometimes brick-wall'd against a rock, so that the guts fly out again; sometimes struck under the wide hazard, and farewell, Master Merchant.

SINDEFY - Well, Frank, well: the seas, you say, are uncertain: but he that sails in your court seas shall find 'em ten times fuller of hazard; wherein to see what is to be seen is torment more than a free spirit can endure; but, when you come to suffer, how many injuries swallow you! What care and devotion must you use to humor an imperious lord, proportion your looks to his looks, smiles to his smiles; fit your sails to the winds of his breath!

QUICKSILVER - Tush! he's no journeyman in his craft that cannot do that.

SINDEFY - But he's worse then a prentice that does it, not only humoring the lord, but every trencher-bearer, every groom that by indulgence and intelligence crept into his favor, and by panderism into his chamber. He rules the roast; and, when my honorable Lord says it shall be thus, my worshipful rascal, the groom of his close-stool, says it shall not be thus, claps the door after him, and who dares enter? A prentice, quoth you? 'T is but to learn to live; and does that disgrace a man? He that rises hardly, stands firmly; but he that rises with ease, alas, falls as easily.

QUICKSILVER - A pox on you! who taught you this morality?

SECURITY - 'T is 'long of this witty age, Master Francis. But, indeed, Mistress Sindefy, all trades complain of inconvenience, and therefore 't is best to have none. The merchant, he complains and says, "Traffic is subject to much uncertainty and loss." Let 'em keep their goods on dry land, with a vengeance, and not expose other men's substances to the mercy of the winds, under protection of a wooden wall, as Master Francis says; and all for greedy desire to enrich themselves with unconscionable gain, two for one, or so; where I, and such other honest men as live by lending money, are content with moderate profit, thirty or forty i' th' hundred, so we may have it with quietness, and out of peril of wind and weather, rather than run those dangerous courses of trading, as they do.

QUICKSILVER - Ay, dad, thou mayst well be called Security, for thou takest the safest course.

SECURITY - Faith, the quieter, and the more contented, and, out of doubt, the more godly; for merchants, in their courses, are never pleas'd, but ever repining against Heaven: one prays for a westerly wind, to carry his ship forth; another for an easterly, to bring his ship home; and, at every shaking of a leaf, he falls into an agony, to think what danger his ship is in on such a coast, and so forth. The farmer, he is ever at odds with the weather: sometimes the clouds have been too barren; sometimes the heavens forget themselves. Their harvests answer not their hopes: sometimes the season falls out too fruitful, corn will bear no price, and so forth. Th' artificer, he's all for a stirring world: if his trade be too dull, and fall short of his expectation, then falls he out of joint. Where we that trade nothing but money are free from all this; we are pleas'd with all weathers. Let it rain or hold up, be calm or windy, let the season be whatsoever, let trade go how it will, we take all in good part, e'en what please the Heavens to send us, so the sun stand not still and the moon keep her usual returns, and make up days, months, and years.

QUICKSILVER - And you have good security!

SECURITY - Ay, marry, Frank, that's the special point.

QUICKSILVER - And yet, forsooth, we must have trades to live withal; for we cannot stand without legs, nor fly without wings, and a number of such scurvy phrases. No, I say still, he that has wit, let him live by his wit; he that has none, let him be a tradesman.

SECURITY - Witty Master Francis! 'T is pity any trade should dull that quick brain of yours. Do but bring knight Petronel into my parchment toils once, and you shall never need to toil in any trade, a' my credit. You know his wife's land?

QUICKSILVER - Even to a foot, sir; I have been often there: a pretty fine seat, good land, all entire within itself.

SECURITY - Well wooded?

QUICKSILVER - Two hundred pounds' worth of wood ready to fell. And a fine sweet house, that stands just in the midst an 't, like a prick in the midst of a circle; would I were your farmer, for a hundred pound a year!

SECURITY - Excellent Master Francis! how I do long to do thee good! How I do hunger and thirst to have the honor to enrich thee! Ay, even to die, that thou mightest inherit my living; even hunger and thirst! For, a' my religion, Master Francis — and so tell knight Petronel — I do it to do him a pleasure.

QUICKSILVER - Marry, dad, his horses are now coming up to bear down his lady; wilt thou lend him thy stable to set 'em in?

SECURITY - Faith, Master Francis, I would be loth to lend my stable out of doors; in a greater matter I will pleasure him, but not in this.

QUICKSILVER - A pox of your hunger and thirst! Well, dad, let him have money; all he could anyway get is bestowed on a ship now bound for Virginia; the frame of which voyage is so closely convey'd that his new lady nor any of her friends know it. Notwithstanding, as soon as his lady's hand is gotten to the sale of her inheritance, and you have furnish'd him with money, he will instantly hoist sail and away.

SECURITY - Now a frank gale of wind go with him, Master Frank! we have too few such knight adventurers! Who would not sell away competent certainties to purchase, with any danger, excellent uncertainties? Your true knight venturer ever does it. Let his wife seal to-day; he shall have his money to-day.

QUICKSILVER - To-morrow she shall, dad, before she goes into the country; to work her to which action with the more engines, I purpose presently to prefer my sweet Sin here to the place of her gentlewoman; whom you, for the more credit, shall present as your friend's daughter, a gentlewoman of the country, new come up with a will for awhile to learn fashions forsooth, and be toward some lady; and she shall buzz pretty devices into her lady's ear; feeding her humors so serviceably, as the manner of such as she is, you know —

SECURITY - True, good Master Francis.

QUICKSILVER - That she shall keep her port open to anything she commends to her.

SECURITY - A' my religion, a most fashionable project; as good she spoil the lady, as the lady spoil her; for 't is three to one of one side. — Sweet Mistress Sin, how are you bound to Master Francis! I do not doubt to see you shortly wed one of the head men of our city.

SINDEFY - But, sweet Frank, when shall my father Security present me?

QUICKSILVER - With all festination; I have broken the ice to it already; and will presently to the knight's house, whither, my good old dad, let me pray thee, with all formality to man her.

SECURITY - Command me, Master Francis; I do hunger and thirst to do thee service! — Come, sweet Mistress Sin, take leave of my Winifred, and we will instantly meet frank Master Francis at your lady's.

Enter WINIFRED above.

WINIFRED - Where is my Cu there? Cu?

SECURITY - Ay, Winnie.

WINIFRED - Wilt thou come in, sweet Cu?

SECURITY - Ay, Winnie, presently.

Exeunt all but QUICKSILVER.

QUICKSILVER - "Ay, Winnie," quod he. That's all he can do, poor man; he may well cut off her name at "Winnie." Oh, 't is an egregious pander! What will not an usurous knave be, so he may be rich? Oh, 't is a notable Jews' trump! I hope to live to see dogs' meat made of the old usurer's flesh, dice of his bones, and indentures of his skin; and yet his skin is too thick to make parchment; 't would make good boots for a peterman to catch salmon in. Your only smooth skin to make fine vellum is your Puritan's skin; they be the smoothest and slickest knaves in a country.

Enter SIR PETRONEL, in boots, with a riding-wand.

SIR PETRONEL - I'll out of this wicked town as fast as my horse can trot! Here's now no good action for a man to spend his time in. Taverns grow dead; ordinaries are blown up; plays are at a stand; houses of hospitality at a fall; not a feather waving, nor a spur jingling anywhere. I'll away instantly.

QUICKSILVER - Y'ad best take some crowns in your purse, knight, or else your Eastward Castle will smoke but miserably.

SIR PETRONEL - Oh, Frank! my castle? Alas! all the castles I have are built with air, thou know'st.

QUICKSILVER - I know it, knight, and therefore wonder whither your lady is going.

SIR PETRONEL - Faith, to seek her fortune, I think. I said I had a castle and land eastward, and eastward she will, without contradiction; her coach and the coach of the sun must meet full butt. And, the sun being outshined with her Ladyship's glory, she fears he goes westward to hang himself.

QUICKSILVER - And I fear, when her enchanted castle becomes invisible, her Ladyship will return and follow his example.

SIR PETRONEL - Oh, that she would have the grace! for I shall never be able to pacify her, when she sees herself deceived so.

QUICKSILVER - As easily as can be. Tell her she mistook your directions, and that shortly yourself will down with her to approve it; and then clothe but her crupper in a new gown, and you may drive her any way you list. For these women, sir, are like Essex calves: you must wriggle 'em on by the tail still, or they will never drive orderly.

SIR PETRONEL - But, alas, sweet Frank! thou know'st my ability will not furnish her blood with those costly humors.

QUICKSILVER - Cast that cost on me, sir. I have spoken to my old pander, Security, for money or commodity; if you will, I know he will procure you.

SIR PETRONEL - Commodity! Alas! what commodity?

QUICKSILVER - Why, sir, what say you to figs and raisins?

SIR PETRONEL - A plague of figs and raisins, and all such frail commodities! We shall make nothing of 'em.

QUICKSILVER - Why then, sir, what say you to forty pound in roasted beef?

SIR PETRONEL - Out upon't. I have less stomach to that than to the figs and raisins. I'll out of town, though I sojourn with a friend of mine; for stay here I must not: my creditors have laid to arrest me, and I have no friend under heaven but my sword to bail me.

QUICKSILVER - God's me, knight, put 'em in sufficient sureties, rather than let your sword bail you! Let 'em take their choice, either the King's Bench or the Fleet, or which of the two Counters they like best, for, by the Lord, I like none of 'em.

SIR PETRONEL - Well, Frank, there is no jesting with my earnest necessity; thou know'st if I make not present money to further my voyage begun, all's lost, and all I have laid out about it.

QUICKSILVER - Why, then, sir, in earnest; if you can get your wise lady to set her hand to the sale of her inheritance, the bloodhound, Security, will smell out ready money for you instantly.

SIR PETRONEL - There spake an angel: to bring her to which conformity, I must fain myself extremely amorous; and, alleging urgent excuses for my stay behind, part with her as passionately as she would from her foisting hound.

QUICKSILVER - You have the sow by the right ear, sir. I warrant there was never child long'd more to ride a cockhorse or wear his new coat than she longs to ride in her new coach. She would long for everything when she was a maid, and now she will run mad for 'em. I lay my life, she will have every year four children; and what charge and change of humor you must endure while she is with child, and how she will tie you to your tackling till she be with child, a dog would not endure. Nay, there is no turnspit dog bound to his wheel more servilely than you shall be to her wheel; for, as that dog can never climb the top of his wheel but when the top comes under him, so shall you never climb the top of her contentment but when she is under you.

SIR PETRONEL - 'Slight, how thou terrifiest me!

QUICKSILVER - Nay, hark you, sir; what nurses, what midwives, what fools, what physicians, what cunning women must be sought for (fearing sometimes she is bewitch'd, sometimes in a consumption), to tell her tales, to talk bawdy to her, to make her laugh, to give her glisters, to let her blood under the tongue and betwixt the toes; how she will revile and kiss you, spit in your face, and lick it off again; how she will vaunt you are her creature; she made you of nothing; how she could have had thousand-mark jointures; she could have been made a lady by a Scotch knight, and never ha' married him; she could have had panadas in her bed every morning; how she set you up, and how she will pull you down — you'll never be able to stand of your legs to endure it.

SIR PETRONEL - Out of my fortune! what a death is my life bound face to face to! The best is, a large time-fitted conscience is bound to nothing: marriage is but a form in the school of policy, to which scholars sit fast'ned only with painted chains. Old Security's young wife is ne'er the further off with me.

QUICKSILVER - Thereby lies a tale, sir. The old usurer will be here instantly, with my punk Sindefy, whom you know your lady has promis'd me to entertain for her gentlewoman; and he, with a purpose to feed on you, invites you most solemnly by me to supper.

SIR PETRONEL - It falls out excellently fitly; I see desire of gain makes jealously venturous.

Enter GERTRUDE.

See, Frank, here comes my lady. Lord, how she views thee! She knows thee not, I think, in this bravery.

GERTRUDE - How now? who be you, I pray?

QUICKSILVER - One Master Francis Quicksilver, an 't please your Ladyship.

GERTRUDE - [aside] God's my dignity! as I am a lady, if he did not make me blush so that mine eyes stood a-water. Would I were unmarried again!—

Enter SECURITY and SINDEFY.

Where's my woman, I pray?

QUICKSILVER - See, madam, she now comes to attend you.

SECURITY - God save my honorable knight and his worshipful lady!

GERTRUDE - Y' are very welcome; you must not put on your hat yet.

SECURITY - No, madam; till I know your Ladyship's further pleasure, I will not presume.

GERTRUDE - And is this a gentleman's daughter new come out of the country?

SECURITY - She is, madam; and one that her father hath a special care to bestow in some honorable lady's service, to put her out of her honest humors, forsooth; for she had a great desire to be a nun, an 't please you.

GERTRUDE - A nun? what nun? a nun substantive? or a nun adjective?

SECURITY - A nun substantive, madam, I hope if a nun be a noun. But, I mean, lady, a vow'd maid of that order.

GERTRUDE - I'll teach her to be a maid of the order, I warrant you. And can you do any work belongs to a lady's chamber?

SINDEFY - What I cannot do, madam, I would be glad to learn.

GERTRUDE - Well said! Hold up, then; hold up your head, I say; come hither a little.

SINDEFY - I thank your Ladyship.

GERTRUDE - And hark you — good man, you may put on your hat now; I do not look on you — I must have you of my faction now; not of my knight's, maid.

SINDEFY - No, forsooth, Madam, of yours.

GERTRUDE - And draw all my servants in my bow, and keep my counsel, and tell me tales, and put me riddles, and read on a book sometimes when I am busy, and laugh at country gentlewomen, and command anything in the house for my retainers; and care not what you spend, for it is all mine; and, in any case, be still a maid, whatsoever you do, or whatsoever any man can do unto you.

SECURITY - I warrant your Ladyship for that.

GERTRUDE - Very well; you shall ride in my coach with me into the country, to-morrow morning. — Come, knight, pray thee let's make a short supper, and to bed presently.

SECURITY - Nay, good madam, this night I have a short supper at home waits on his Worship's acceptation.

GERTRUDE - By my faith, but he shall not go, sir; I shall swoon an he sup from me.

SIR PETRONEL - Pray thee, forbear; shall he lose his provision?

GERTRUDE - Ay, by'r Lady, sir, rather than I lose my longing. Come in, I say; as I am a lady, you shall not go.

QUICKSILVER - [aside] I told him what a burr he had gotten.

SECURITY - If you will not sup from your knight, madam, let me entreat your Ladyship to sup at my house with him.

GERTRUDE - No, by my faith, sir; then we cannot be abed soon enough after supper.

SIR PETRONEL - [aside] What a med'cine is this! — Well, Master Security, you are new married as well as I; I hope you are bound as well. We must honor our young wives, you know.

QUICKSILVER - [aside to SECURITY] In policy, dad, till to-morrow she has seal'd.

SECURITY - I hope in the morning yet your Knighthood will breakfast with me.

SIR PETRONEL - As early as you will, sir.

SECURITY - Thank your good Worship; I do hunger and thirst to do you good, sir!

GERTRUDE - Come, sweet knight, come; I do hunger and thirst to be abed with thee!

Exeunt.

ACT III — SCENE I – THE SAME

Enter PETRONEL, QUICKSILVER, SECURITY, BRAMBLE, and WINIFRED.

SIR PETRONEL - Thanks for our feastlike breakfast, good Master Security; I am sorry, by reason of my instant haste to so long a voyage as Virginia, I am without means by any kind amends to show how affectionately I take your kindness, and to confirm by some worthy ceremony a perpetual league of friendship betwixt us.

SECURITY - Excellent knight! let this be a token betwixt us of inviolable friendship. I am new married to this fair gentlewoman, you know; and, by my hope to make her fruitful, though I be something in years, I vow faithfully unto you to make you godfather, though in your absence, to the first child I am blest withal; and henceforth call me gossip, I beseech you, if you please to accept it.

SIR PETRONEL - In the highest degree of gratitude, my most worthy gossip; for confirmation of which friendly title, let me entreat my fair gossip, your wife here, to accept this diamond, and keep it as my gift to her first child, wheresoever my fortune, in event of my voyage, shall bestow me.

SECURITY - How now, my coy wedlock! Make you strange of so noble a favor? Take it, I charge you, with all affection, and, by way of taking your leave, present boldly your lips to our honorable gossip.

QUICKSILVER - [aside] How vent'rous he is to him, and how jealous to others!

SIR PETRONEL - Long may this kind touch of our lips print in our hearts all the forms of affection. — And now, my good gossip, if the writings be ready to which my wife should seal, let them be brought this morning before she takes coach into the country, and my kindness shall work her to dispatch it.

SECURITY - The writings are ready, sir. My learned counsel here, Master Bramble the lawyer, hath perus'd them; and within this hour I will bring the scrivener with them to your worshipful lady.

SIR PETRONEL - Good Master Bramble, I will here take my leave of you, then. God send you fortunate pleas, sir, and contentious clients!

Exit.

BRAMBLE - And you foreright winds, sir, and a fortunate voyage.

Enter a MESSENGER.

MESSENGER - Sir Petronel, here are three or four gentlemen desire to speak with you.

SIR PETRONEL - What are they?

QUICKSILVER - They are your followers in this voyage, knight: Captain Seagull and his associates; I met them this morning, and told them you would be here.

SIR PETRONEL - Let them enter, I pray you; I know they long to be gone, for their stay is dangerous.

Enter SEAGULL, SCAPETHRIFT, and SPENDALL.

SEAGULL - God save my honorable colonel!

SIR PETRONEL - Welcome, good Captain Seagull and worthy gentlemen. If you will meet my friend Frank here and me at the Blue Anchor Tavern by Billingsgate this evening, we will there drink to our happy voyage, be merry, and take boat to our ship with all expedition.

SEAGULL - Defer it no longer, I beseech you, sir; but, as your voyage is hitherto carried closely, and in another knight's name, so for your own safety and ours, let it be continued; our meeting and speedy purpose of departing known to as few as is possible, lest your ship and goods be attach'd.

QUICKSILVER - Well advis'd, captain; our colonel shall have money this morning, to dispatch all our departures. Bring those gentlemen at night to the place appointed, and, with our skins full of vintage, we'll take occasion by the vantage, and away.

SPENDALL - We will not fail but be there, sir.

SIR PETRONEL - Good morrow, good Captain, and my worthy associates. — Health and all sovereignty to my beautiful gossip! — For you, sir, we shall see you presently with the writings.

SECURITY - With writings and crowns to my honorable gossip. I do hunger and thirst to do you good, sir.

Exeunt.

SCENE II – AN INNYARD

Enter a COACHMAN in haste, in 's frock, feeding.

COACHMAN - Here's a stir when citizens ride out of town, indeed, as if all the house were afire! 'Slight! they will not give a man leave to eat 's breakfast afore he rises.

Enter HAMLET, a footman, in haste.

HAMLET - What, coachman! My Lady's coach, for shame! Her Ladyship's ready to come down.

Enter POTKIN, a tankard-bearer.

POTKIN - 'Sfoot, Hamlet, are you mad? Whither run you now? You should brush up my old mistress!

Exit HAMLET.

Enter SINDEFY.

SINDEFY - What, Potkin! You must put off your tankard and put on your blue coat, and wait upon Mistress Touchstone into the country.

Exit.

POTKIN - I will, forsooth, presently.

Enter MISTRESS FOND and MISTRESS GAZER.

MISTRESS FOND - Come, sweet Mistress Gazer, let's watch here, and see my Lady Flash take coach.

MISTRESS GAZER - A' my word, here's a most fine place to stand in; did you see the new ship launch'd last day, Mistress Fond?

MISTRESS FOND - O God! an we citizens should lose such a sight!

MISTRESS GAZER - I warrant here will be double as many people to see her take coach as there were to see it take water.

MISTRESS FOND - Oh, she's married to a most fine castle i' th' country, they say!

MISTRESS GAZER - But there are no giants in the castle, are there?

MISTRESS FOND - Oh, no; they say her knight kill'd 'em all; and therefore he was knighted.

MISTRESS GAZER - Would to God her Ladyship would come away!

Enter GERTRUDE, MISTRESS TOUCHSTONE, SINDEFY, HAMLET, and POTKIN.

MISTRESS FOND - She comes, she comes, she comes!

MISTRESS GAZER and MISTRESS FOND - Pray Heaven bless your Ladyship!

GERTRUDE - Thank you, good people! — My coach, for the love of Heaven, my coach! In good truth I shall swoon else.

HAMLET - Coach, coach, my Lady's coach!

Exit.

GERTRUDE - As I am a lady, I think I am with child already, I long for a coach so. May one be with child afore they are married, Mother?

MISTRESS TOUCHSTONE - Ay, by'r Lady, madam; a little thing does that: I have seen a little prick no bigger then a pin's head swell bigger and bigger, till it has come to an ancome; and e'en so 't is in these cases.

Re-enter HAMLET.

HAMLET - Your coach is coming, madam.

GERTRUDE - That's well said. — Now, Heaven! methinks I am e'en up to the knees in preferment. [singing]
But a little higher, but a little higher, but a little higher,
There, there, there lies Cupid's fire!

MISTRESS TOUCHSTONE - But must this young man, an 't please you, madam, run by your coach all the way afoot?

GERTRUDE - Ay, by my faith, I warrant him; he gives no other milk, as I have another servant does.

MISTRESS TOUCHSTONE - Alas! 't is e'en pity, methinks; for God's sake, madam, buy him but a hobby-horse; let the poor youth have something betwixt his legs to ease 'em. Alas! we must do as we would be done to.

GERTRUDE - Go to, hold your peace, dame; you talk like an old fool, I tell you!

Enter PETRONEL and QUICKSILVER.

SIR PETRONEL - Wilt thou be gone, sweet honeysuckle, before I can go with thee?

GERTRUDE - I pray thee, sweet knight, let me; I do so long to dress up thy castle afore thou com'st. But I mar'l how my modest sister occupies herself this morning, that she cannot wait on me to my coach, as well as her mother.

QUICKSILVER - Marry, madam, she's married by this time to prentice Golding. Your father, and someone more, stole to church with 'em in all the haste, that the cold meat left at your wedding might serve to furnish their nuptial table.

GERTRUDE - There's no base fellow, my father, now; but he's e'en fit to father such a daughter. He must call me "daughter" no more now: but "madam," and "please you, madam"; and "please your Worship, madam," indeed. Out upon him! marry his daughter to a base prentice?

MISTRESS TOUCHSTONE - What should one do? Is there no law for one that marries a woman's daughter against her will? How shall we punish him, madam?

GERTRUDE - As I am a lady, an 't would snow, we'd so pebble 'em with snowballs as they come from church; but, sirrah Frank Quicksilver —

QUICKSILVER - Ay, madam.

GERTRUDE - Dost remember since thou and I clapp'd what-d'ye-call'ts in the garret?

QUICKSILVER - I know not what you mean, madam.

GERTRUDE - [singing]
His head as white as milk,
All flaxen was his hair;
But now he is dead,
And laid in his bed,
And never will come again.

God be at your labor!

Enter TOUCHSTONE, GOLDING, and MILDRED with rosemary.

SIR PETRONEL - [aside] Was there ever such a lady?

QUICKSILVER - See, madam, the bride and bridegroom!

GERTRUDE - God's my precious! God give you joy, Mistress What-lack-you! Now out upon thee, baggage! My sister married in a taffeta hat! Marry, hang you! Westward with a wanion t' ye! Nay, I have done wi' ye, minion, then, i' faith; never look to have my countenance any more, nor anything I can do for thee. Thou ride in my coach, or come down to my castle? fie upon thee! I charge thee in my Ladyship's name, call me "sister" no more.

TOUCHSTONE - An 't please your Worship, this is not your sister: this is my daughter, and she calls me "Father," and so does not your Ladyship, an 't please your Worship, madam.

MISTRESS TOUCHSTONE - No, nor she must not call thee father by heraldry, because thou mak'st thy prentice thy son as well as she. Ah, thou misproud prentice! dar'st thou presume to marry a lady's sister?

GOLDING - It pleas'd my master, forsooth, to embolden me with his favor; and, though I confess myself far unworthy so worthy a wife, being in part her servant, as I am your prentice, yet, since (I may say it without boasting) I am born a gentleman, and, by the trade I have learn'd of my master, which I trust taints not my blood, able, with mine own industry and portion, to maintain your daughter, my hope is Heaven will so bless our humble beginning that in the end I shall be no disgrace to the grace with which my master hath bound me his double prentice.

TOUCHSTONE - Master me no more, son, if thou think'st me worthy to be thy father.

GERTRUDE - "Sun"? Now, good Lord, how he shines, an you mark him! He's a gentleman!

GOLDING - Ay, indeed, madam, a gentleman born.

SIR PETRONEL - Never stand a' your gentry, Master Bridegroom; if your legs be no better than your arms, you'll be able to stand upon neither shortly.

TOUCHSTONE - An 't please your good Worship, sir, there are two sorts of gentlemen.

SIR PETRONEL - What mean you, sir?

TOUCHSTONE - Bold to put off my hat to your Worship—

SIR PETRONEL - Nay, pray forbear, sir, and then forth with your two sorts of gentlemen.

TOUCHSTONE - If your Worship will have it so! — I say there are two sorts of gentlemen. There is a gentleman artificial, and a gentleman natural. Now, though your Worship be a gentleman natural — work upon that now!

QUICKSILVER - Well said, old Touchstone; I am proud to hear thee enter a set speech, i' faith; forth, I beseech thee.

TOUCHSTONE - Cry you mercy, sir, your Worship's a gentleman I do not know. If you be one of my acquaintance, y' are very much disguis'd, sir.

QUICKSILVER - Go to, old quipper; forth with thy speech, I say.

TOUCHSTONE - What, sir, my speeches were ever in vain to your gracious Worship; and therefore, till I speak to you gallantry indeed I will save my breath for my broth anon. Come, my poor son and daughter, let us hide ourselves in our poor humility, and live safe. Ambition consumes itself with the very show. Work upon that now!

Exeunt TOUCHSTONE, GOLDING and MILDRED.

GERTRUDE - Let him go, let him go, for God's sake! let him make his prentice his son, for God's sake! give away his daughter, for God's sake! and when they come a-begging to us, for God's sake, let's laugh at their good husbandry for God's sake. Farewell, sweet knight, pray thee make haste after.

SIR PETRONEL - What shall I say? I would not have thee go.

QUICKSILVER - [singing]
Now, oh, now, I must depart;
Parting, though it absence move —

This ditty, knight, do I see in thy looks in capital letters. —
[singing]
What a grief 'tis to depart, and leave the flower that has my heart!
My sweet lady, and, alack for woe, why should we part so?

Tell truth, knight, and shame all dissembling lovers; does not your pain lie on that side?

SIR PETRONEL - If it do, canst thou tell me how I may cure it?

QUICKSILVER - Excellent easily. Divide yourself in two halves, just by the girdlestead; send one half with your lady, and keep the tother yourself; or else do as all true lovers do, part with your heart and leave your body behind. I have seen 't done a hundred times: 't is as easy a matter for a lover to part without a heart from his sweetheart, and he ne'er the worse, as for a mouse to get from a trap and leave her tail behind her. See, here comes the writings.

Enter SECURITY, with a SCRIVENER.

SECURITY - Good morrow to my worshipful Lady. I present your Ladyship with this writing, to which, if you please to set your hand with your knight's, a velvet gown shall attend your journey, a' my credit.

GERTRUDE - What writing is it, knight?

SIR PETRONEL - The sale, sweetheart, of the poor tenement I told thee of, only to make a little money to send thee down furniture for my castle, to which my hand shall lead thee.

GERTRUDE - Very well. Now give me your pen, I pray.

QUICKSILVER - [aside] It goes down without chewing, i' faith.

SCRIVENER - Your Worships deliver this as your deed?

OMNES - We do.

GERTRUDE - So now, knight, farewell till I see thee!

SIR PETRONEL - All farewell to my sweetheart.

MISTRESS TOUCHSTONE - Good-bye, son knight.

SIR PETRONEL - Farewell, my good mother!

GERTRUDE - Farewell, Frank! I would fain take thee down if I could.

QUICKSILVER - I thank your good Ladyship. — Farewell, Mistress Sindefy!

Exeunt GERTRUDE and her party.

SIR PETRONEL - O tedious voyage, whereof there is no end!
What will they think of me?

QUICKSILVER - Think what they list. They long'd for a vagary into the country; and now they are fitted. So a woman marry to ride in a coach, she cares not if she ride to her ruin. 'T is the great end of many of their marriages. This is not first time a lady has rid a false journey in her coach, I hope.

SIR PETRONEL - Nay, 't is no matter, I care little what they think; he that weighs men's thoughts has his hands full of nothing. A man, in the course of this world, should be like a surgeon's instrument, work in the wounds of others, and feel nothing himself. The sharper and subtler, the better.

QUICKSILVER - As it falls out now, knight, you shall not need to devise excuses, or endure her outcries, when she returns; we shall now be gone before, where they can not reach us.

SIR PETRONEL - Well, my kind compere, you have now th' assurance we both can make you; let me now entreat you the money we agreed on may be brought to the Blue Anchor, near to Billingsgate, by six a'clock; where I and my chief friends, bound for this voyage, will with feasts attend you.

SECURITY - The money, my most honorable compere, shall without fail observe your appointed hour.

SIR PETRONEL - Thanks, my dear gossip. I must now impart
To your approved love a loving secret,
As one on whom my life doth more rely
In friendly trust than any man alive.
Nor shall you be the chosen secretary
Of my affections for affection only;
For I protest, if God bless my return,
To make you partner in my action's gain
As deeply as if you had ventur'd with me
Half my expenses. Know then, honest gossip,
I have enjoyed with such divine contentment
A gentlewoman's bed whom you well know,
That I shall ne'er enjoy this tedious voyage,
Nor live the least part of the time it asketh,
Without her presence; so "I thirst and hunger"
To taste the dear feast of her company.
And, if the "hunger" and "the thirst" you vow
As my sworn gossip, to my wished good
Be, as I know it is, unfeign'd and firm,
Do me an easy favor in your power.

SECURITY - Be sure, brave gossip, all that I can do,
To my best nerve, is wholly at your service.
Who is the woman, first, that is your friend?

SIR PETRONEL - The woman is your learned counsel's wife,
The lawyer, Master Bramble; whom would you
Bring out this even in honest neighborhood,
To take his leave, with you, of me your gossip,
I, in the mean time, will send this my friend
Home to his house, to bring his wife, disguis'd,
Before his face, into our company;
For love hath made her look for such a wile,
To free her from his tyrannous jealousy;
And I would take this course before another,
In stealing her away, to make us sport,
And gull his circumspection the more grossly;
And I am sure that no man like yourself
Hath credit with him to entice his jealousy
To so long stay abroad as may give time
To her enlargement in such safe disguise.

SECURITY - A pretty, pithy, and most pleasant project!
Who would not strain a point of neighborhood
For such a point-device? — that, as the ship

Of famous Draco went about the world,
Will wind about the lawyer, compassing
The world, himself; he hath it in his arms,
And that's enough for him, without his wife.
A lawyer is ambitious, and his head
Cannot be prais'd nor rais'd too high,
With any fork of highest knavery.
I'll go fetch him straight.

Exit SECURITY.

SIR PETRONEL - So, so! Now, Frank, go thou home to his house,
'Stead of his lawyer's, and bring his wife hither,
Who, just like to the lawyer's wife, is prison'd
With his stern usurous jealousy, which could never
Be overreach'd thus but with overreaching.

Re-enter SECURITY.

SECURITY - And, Master Francis, watch you th' instant time
To enter with his exit: 't will be rare,

Exit.

Two fine horn'd beasts, a camel and a lawyer!

QUICKSILVER - How the old villain joys in villainy!

Re-enter SECURITY.

SECURITY - And hark you, gossip, when you have her here,
Have your boat ready, ship her to your ship
With utmost haste, lest Master Bramble stay you.
To o'erreach that head that outreacheth all heads!
'T is a trick rampant! — 't is a very quibblin!
I hope this harvest to pitch cart with lawyers,
Their heads will be so forked. This sly touch
Will get apes to invent a number such.

Exit.

QUICKSILVER - Was ever rascal honeyed so with poison?
"He that delights in slavish avarice,
Is apt to joy in every sort of vice."
Well, I'll go fetch his wife, whilst he the lawyer.

SIR PETRONEL - But stay, Frank, let's think how we may disguise her.
Upon this sudden.

QUICKSILVER - God's me, there's the mischief!
But hark you, here's an excellent device —

'Fore God, a rare one! I will carry her
A sailor's gown and cap, and cover her,
And a player's beard.

SIR PETRONEL - And what upon her head?

QUICKSILVER - I tell you, a sailor's cap! 'Slight, God forgive me!
What kind of figent memory have you?

SIR PETRONEL - Nay, then, what kind of figent wit hast thou?
A sailor's cap? — how shall she put it off
When thou present'st her to our company?

QUICKSILVER - Tush, man, for that, make her a saucy sailor!

SIR PETRONEL - Tush, tush! 't is no fit sauce for such sweet mutton.
I know not what t' advise.

Enter SECURITY with his wife's gown.

SECURITY - Knight, knight, a rare device!

SIR PETRONEL - Sownes, yet again?

QUICKSILVER - What stratagem have you now?

SECURITY - The best that ever — you talk'd of disguising?

SIR PETRONEL - Ay, marry, gossip, that's our present care.

SECURITY - Cast care away then; here's the best device
For plain Security (for I am no better),
I think, that ever liv'd; here's my wife's gown,
Which you may put upon the lawyer's wife,
And which I brought you, sir, for two great reasons:
One is, that Master Bramble may take hold
Of some suspicion that it is my wife,
And gird me so perhaps with his law wit;
The other, which is policy indeed,
Is that my wife may now be tied at home,
Having no more but her old gown abroad,
And not show me a quirk, while I firk others.
Is not this rare?

SIR PETRONEL - The best that ever was.

SECURITY - Am I not born to furnish gentlemen?

SIR PETRONEL - O my dear gossip!

SECURITY - Well, hold, Master Francis;

Watch, when the lawyer's out, and put it in.

Exit.

And now — I will go fetch him.

QUICKSILVER - O my dad!
He goes as 't were the Devil to fetch the lawyer;
And devil shall he be, if horns will make him.

Re-enter SECURITY.

SIR PETRONEL - Why, how now, gossip? why stay you there musing?

SECURITY - A toy, a toy runs in my head, i' faith.

QUICKSILVER - A pox of that head! is there more toys yet?

SIR PETRONEL - What is it, pray thee, gossip?

SECURITY - Why, sir, what if you
Should slip away now with my wife's best gown,
I having no security for it?

QUICKSILVER - For that, I hope, dad, you will take our words.

SECURITY - Ay, by th' mass, your word; that's a proper staff
For wise Security to lean upon!
But 't is no matter; once I'll trust my name
On your crack'd credits; let it take no shame.

Exit.

Fetch the wench, Frank.

QUICKSILVER - I'll wait upon you, sir. —
And fetch you over, you were ne'er so fetch'd.
Go to the tavern, knight; your followers

Exit.

Dare not be drunk, I think, before their captain.

SIR PETRONEL - Would I might lead them to no hotter service
Till our Virginian gold were in our purses!

Exit.

SCENE III – A ROOM IN THE BLUE ANCHOR TAVERN

Enter SEAGULL, SPENDALL, and SCAPETHRIFT, in the tavern, with a DRAWER.

SEAGULL - Come, drawer, pierce your neatest hogsheads, and let's have cheer, not fit for your Billingsgate tavern, but for our Virginian colonel; he will be here instantly.

DRAWER - You shall have all things fit, sir; please you have any more wine?

SPENDALL - More wine, slave! Whether we drink it or no, spill it, and draw more.

SCAPETHRIFT - Fill all the pots in your house with all sorts of liquor, and let 'em wait on us here like soldiers in their pewter coats; and, though we do not employ them now, yet we will maintain 'em till we do.

DRAWER - Said like an honorable captain; you shall have all you can command, sir.

Exit DRAWER.

SEAGULL - Come, boys, Virginia longs till we share the rest of her maidenhead.

SPENDALL - Why, is she inhabited already with any English?

SEAGULL - A whole country of English is there, man, bred of those that were left there in '79; they have married with the Indians, and make 'em bring forth as beautiful faces as any we have in England; and therefore the Indians are so in love with 'em that all the treasure they have they lay at their feet.

SCAPETHRIFT - But is there such treasure there, Captain, as I have heard?

SEAGULL - I tell thee, gold is more plentiful there than copper is with us; and for as much red copper as I can bring, I'll have thrice the weight in Gold. Why, man, all their dripping-pans and their chamber pots are pure gold; and all their chains with which they chain up their streets are massy gold; all the prisoners they take are fetter'd in gold; and, for rubies and diamonds, they go forth on holidays and gather 'em by the seashore, to hang on their children's coats, and stick in their caps, as commonly as our children wear saffron gilt brooches and groats with holes in 'em.

SCAPETHRIFT - And is it a pleasant country withal?

SEAGULL - As ever the sun shin'd on; temperate, and full of all sorts of excellent viands: wild boar is as common there as our tamest bacon is here; venison, as mutton. And then you shall live freely there, without sergeants, or courtiers, or lawyers, or intelligencers, only a few industrious Scots, perhaps, who indeed are dispers'd over the face of the whole earth. But, as for them, there are no greater friends to Englishmen and England, when they are out on't, in the world, than they are. And, for my part, I would a hundred thousand of 'em were there, for we are all one countrymen now, ye know; and we should find ten times more comfort of them there than we do here. Then, for your means to advancement there, it is simple, and not preposterously mix'd. You may be an alderman there, and never be scavenger; you may be a nobleman, and never be a slave. You may come to preferment enough, and never be a pander; to riches and fortune enough, and have never the more villainy nor the less wit.

SPENDALL - Gods me! and how far is it thither?

SEAGULL - Some six weeks' sail, no more, with any indifferent good wind. And, if I get to any part of the coast of Africa, I'll sail thither with any wind; or, when I come to Cape Finisterre, there's a foreright wind continually wafts us till we come at Virginia. — See, our colonel's come.

Enter SIR PETRONEL.

SIR PETRONEL - Well met, good Captain Seagull and my noble gentlemen! Now the sweet hour of our freedom is at hand. — Come, drawer! Fill us some carouses, and prepare us for the mirth that will be occasioned presently. Here will be a pretty wench, gentlemen, that will bear us company all our voyage.

SEAGULL - Whatsoever she be, here's to her health, noble colonel, both with cap and knee.

SIR PETRONEL - Thanks, kind Captain Seagull; she's one I love dearly and must not be known, till we be free from all that know us. And so, gentlemen, here's to her health.

SEAGULL - Let it come, worthy Colonel; we do hunger and thirst for it!

SIR PETRONEL - Afore Heaven, you have hit the phrase of one that her presence will touch from the foot to the forehead, if ye knew it.

SPENDALL - Why, then, we will join his forehead with her health, sir; and, Captain Scapethrift, here's to 'em both.

Enter SECURITY and BRAMBLE.

SECURITY - See, see, Master Bramble, 'fore Heaven, their voyage cannot but prosper! they are o' their knees for success to it!

BRAMBLE - And they pray to god Bacchus.

SECURITY - God save my brave colonel, with all his tall captains and corporals. See, sir, my worshipful learned counsel, Master Bramble, is come to take his leave of you.

SIR PETRONEL - Worshipful Master Bramble, how far do you draw us into the sweet briar of your kindness! — Come, Captain Seagull, another health to this rare Bramble, that hath never a prick about him.

SEAGULL - I pledge his most smooth disposition, sir. — Come, Master Security, bend your supporters, and pledge this notorious health here.

SECURITY - Bend you yours likewise, Master Bramble; for it is you shall pledge me.

SEAGULL - Not so, Master Security; he must not pledge his own health.

SECURITY - No, Master Captain?

Enter QUICKSILVER, with WINNIFRED, disguis'd.

Why, then, here's one is fitly come to do him that honor.

QUICKSILVER - Here's the gentlewoman your cousin, sir, whom, with much entreaty, I have brought to take her leave of you in a tavern; asham'd whereof, you must pardon her if she put not off her mask.

SIR PETRONEL - Pardon me, sweet Cousin; my kind desire to see you before I went made me so importunate to entreat your presence here.

SECURITY - How now, Master Francis, have you honor'd this presence with a fair gentlewoman?

QUICKSILVER - Pray, sir, take you no notice of her, for she will not be known to you.

SECURITY - But my learned counsel, Master Bramble here, I hope may know her.

QUICKSILVER - No more than you, sir, at this time; his learning must pardon her.

SECURITY - Well, God pardon her, for my part; and I do, I'll be sworn. And so, Master Francis, here's to all that are going eastward to-night towards Cuckold's Haven; and so to the health of Master Bramble.

QUICKSILVER - I pledge it, sir.

[Kneeling]

Hath it gone round, captains?

SEAGULL - It has, sweet Frank; and the round closes with thee.

QUICKSILVER - Well, sir, here's to all eastward and toward cuckolds, and so to famous Cuckold's Haven, so fatally rememb'red. Surgit.

SIR PETRONEL - [to WINIFRED] Nay, pray thee, coz, weep not. — Gossip Security.

SECURITY - Ay, my brave gossip.

SIR PETRONEL - A word, I beseech you, sir. — [aside] Our friend, Mistress Bramble here, is so dissolv'd in tears, that she drowns the whole mirth of our meeting. Sweet gossip, take her aside and comfort her.

SECURITY - [aside to WINIFRED] Pity of all true love, Mistress Bramble; what, weep you to enjoy your love? What's the cause, lady? Is 't because your husband is so near, and your heart earns to have a little abus'd him? Alas, alas! the offence is too common to be respected. So great a grace hath seldom chanc'd to so unthankful a woman; to be rid of an old jealous dotard, to enjoy the arms of a loving young knight, that, when your prickless Bramble is withered with grief of your loss, will make you flourish afresh in the bed of a lady.

Re-enter DRAWER.

DRAWER - Sir Petronel, here's one of your watermen come to tell you it will be flood these three hours; and that 't will be dangerous going against the tide; for the sky is overcast, and there was a porpoise even now seen at London Bridge, which is always the messenger of tempests, he says.

SIR PETRONEL - A porpoise! — what's that to th' purpose? Charge him, if he love his life, to attend us. Can we not reach Blackwall, where my ship lies, against the tide, and in spite of tempests? Captains and gentlemen, we'll begin a new ceremony at the beginning of our voyage, which I believe will be follow'd of all future adventurers.

SEAGULL - What's that, good Colonel?

SIR PETRONEL - This, Captain Seagull. We'll have our provided supper brought aboard Sir Francis Drake's ship, that hath compass'd the world; where, with full cups and banquets, we will do sacrifice for a prosperous voyage. My mind gives me that some good spirits of the waters should haunt the desert ribs of her, and be auspicious to all that honor her memory, and will with like orgies enter their voyages.

SEAGULL - Rarely conceited! One health more to this motion, and aboard to perform it. He that will not this night be drunk, may he never be sober.

They compass in WINIFRED, dance the drunken round, and drink carouses.

BRAMBLE - Sir Petronel and his honorable captains, in these young services we old servitors may be spar'd. We only came to take our leaves, and, with one health to you all, I'll be bold to do so. Here, neighbor Security, to the health of Sir Petronel and all his captains.

SECURITY - You must bend, then, Master Bramble. [They kneel.] So, now I am for you. I have one corner of my brain, I hope, fit to bear one carouse more. Here, lady, to you that are encompass'd there, and are asham'd of our company. [They drink, and rise.] Ha, ha, ha! by my troth, my learn'd counsel, Master Bramble, my mind runs so of Cuckold's Haven to-night that my head runs over with admiration.

BRAMBLE - [aside to SECURITY] But is not that your wife, neighbor?

SECURITY - [aside to BRAMBLE.] No, by my troth, Master Bramble. Ha, ha, ha! A pox of all Cuckold's Havens, I say!

BRAMBLE - [aside to SECURITY] A' my faith, her garments are exceeding like your wife's.

SECURITY - Cucullus non facit monachum, my learned counsel; all are not cuckolds that seem so; nor all seem not that are so. Give me your hand, my learn'd counsel; you and I will sup somewhere else than at Sir Francis Drake's ship to-night. — Adieu, my noble gossip!

BRAMBLE - Good fortune, brave captains; fair skies God send ye!

OMNES - Farewell, my hearts, farewell!

SIR PETRONEL - Gossip, laugh no more at Cuckold's Haven, gossip.

SECURITY - I have done, I have done, sir. — Will you lead, Master Bramble? Ha, ha, ha!

SIR PETRONEL - Captain Seagull, charge a boat.

OMNES - A boat, a boat, a boat!

Exeunt all except DRAWER.

DRAWER - Y' are in a proper taking indeed, to take a boat, especially at this time of night, and against tide and tempest. They say yet, "Drunken men never take harm." This night will try the truth of that proverb.

Exit.

Enter SECURITY.

SECURITY - What, Winnie! — Wife, I say! — Outdoors at this time! Where should I seek the gadfly? — Billingsgate, Billingsgate, Billingsgate! She's gone with the knight, she's gone with the knight! woe be to thee, Billingsgate! — A boat! a boat! a boat! a full hundred marks for a boat!

Exit.

Enter SLITGUT with a pair of ox-horns, discovering Cuckold's Haven above.

SLITGUT - All hail, fair haven of married men only! for there are none but married men cuckolds. For my part, I presume not to arrive here but in my master's behalf, a poor butcher of Eastcheap, who sends me to set up, in honor of Saint Luke, these necessary ensigns of his homage. And up I got this morning, thus early, to get up to the top of this famous tree, that is all fruit and no leaves, to advance this crest of my master's occupation. Up then! — Heaven and Saint Luke bless me, that I be not blown into the Thames as I climb, with this furious tempest. 'Slight! I think the Devil be abroad, in likeness of a storm, to rob me of my horns! Hark how he roars! Lord! what a coil the Thames keeps! She bears some unjust burthen, I believe, that she kicks and curvets thus to cast it. Heaven bless all honest passengers that are upon her back now; for the bit is out of her mouth, I see, and she will run away with 'em! — So, so! I think I have made it look the right way. — It runs against London Bridge, as it were, even full butt. And now let me discover from this lofty prospect, what pranks the rude Thames plays in her desperate lunacy. O me! here's a boat has been cast away hard by. Alas, alas, see one of her passengers laboring for his life to land at this haven here! Pray Heaven he may recover it! His next land is even just under me. — Hold out yet a little; whatsoever thou art, pray, and take a good heart to thee. — 'T is a man; — take a man's heart to thee; yet a little further, get up a' thy legs, man; now 't is shallow enough. So, so, so! Alas! he's down again. Hold thy wind, father. — 'T is a man in a nightcap. So! now he's got up again; now he's past the worst: yet, thanks be to Heaven, he comes toward me pretty and strongly.

Enter SECURITY, without his hat, in a nightcap, wet band, etc.

SECURITY - Heaven, I beseech thee, how have I offended thee! where am I cast ashore now, that I may go a righter way home by land? Let me see; Oh, I am scarce able to look about me. Where is there any sea-mark that I am acquainted withal?

SLITGUT - Look up, father; are you acquainted with this mark?

SECURITY - What! landed at Cuckold's Haven? Hell and damnation! I will run back and drown myself.

He falls down.

SLITGUT - Poor man, how weak he is! the weak water has wash'd away his strength.

SECURITY - Landed at Cuckold's Haven! If it had not been to die twenty times alive, I should never have 'scap'd death! I will never arise more; I will grovel here and eat dirt till I be chok'd; I will make the gentle earth do that which the cruel water has denied me.

SLITGUT - Alas, good father, be not so desperate! Rise man; if you will, I'll come presently and lead you home.

SECURITY - Home! shall I make any know my home that has known me thus abroad? How low shall I crouch away, that no eye may see me? I will creep on the earth while I live, and never look heaven in the face more.

Exit, creeping.

SLITGUT - What young planet reigns now, trow, that old men are so foolish? What desperate young swaggerer would have been abroad such a weather as this, upon the water? — Ay me, see another remnant of this unfortunate shipwrack! — or some other. A woman, i' faith, a woman; though it be almost at Saint Kath'rine's, I discern it to be a woman, for all her body is above the water, and her clothes swim about her most handsomely. Oh, they bear her up most bravely! Has not a woman reason to love the taking up of her clothes the better while she lives, for this? Alas, how busy the rude Thames is about her! A pox a' that wave! It will drown her, i' faith, 't will drown her! Cry God mercy, she has scap'd it! I thank Heaven she has scap'd it! Oh, how she swims, like a mermaid! Some vigilant body look out and save her. That's well said; just where the priest fell in, there's one sets down a ladder, and goes to take her up. God's blessing a' thy heart, boy! Now take her up in thy arms and to bed with her. She's up, she's up! She's a beautiful woman, I warrant her; the billows durst not devour her.

Enter the DRAWER in the tavern before, with WINIFRED.

DRAWER - How fare you now, lady?

WINIFRED - Much better, my good friend, than I wish: as one desperate of her fame, now my life is preserv'd.

DRAWER - Comfort yourself. That Power that preserved you from death can likewise defend you from infamy, howsoever you deserve it. Were not you one that took boat late this night, with a knight and other gentlemen at Billingsgate?

WINIFRED - Unhappy that I am, I was.

DRAWER - I am glad it was my good hap to come down thus far after you, to a house of my friends here in Saint Kath'rine's, since I am now happily made a mean to your rescue from the ruthless tempest, which, when you took boat, was so extreme, and the gentleman that brought you forth so desperate and unsober, that I fear'd long ere this I should hear of your shipwreck, and therefore, with little other reason, made thus far this way. And this I must tell you, since perhaps you may make use of it, there was left behind you at our tavern, brought by a porter hir'd by the young gentleman that brought you, a gentlewoman's gown, hat, stockings, and shoes; which, if they be yours, and you please to shift you, taking a hard bed here in this house of my friend, I will presently go fetch you.

WINIFRED - Thanks, my good friend, for your more than good news. The gown with all things bound with it are mine; which if you please to fetch as you have promis'd, I will boldly receive the kind favor you have offered till your return; entreating you, by all the good you have done in preserving me hitherto, to let none take knowledge of what favor you do me, or where such a one as I am bestowed, lest you incur me much more damage in my fame than you have done me pleasure in preserving my life.

DRAWER - Come in, lady, and shift yourself; resolve that nothing but your own pleasure shall be us'd in your discovery.

WINIFRED - Thank you, good friend; the time may come, I shall requite you.

Exeunt Drawer and WINIFRED.

SLITGUT - See, see, see! I hold my life, there's some other a-taking up at Wapping now! Look, what a sort of people cluster about the gallows there! in good troth, it is so. O me! a fine young gentleman! What, and taken up at the gallows? Heaven grant he be not one day taken down there! A' my life, it is ominous. Well, he is delivered for the time. I see the people have all left him; yet will I keep my prospect awhile, to see if any more have been shipwrack'd.

Enter QUICKSILVER, bareheaded.

QUICKSILVER - Accurs'd that ever I was sav'd or born!
How fatal is my sad arrival here!
As if the stars and Providence spake to me,
And said, "The drift of all unlawful courses,
Whatever end they dare propose themselves,
In frame of their licentious policies,
In the firm order of just destiny,
They are the ready highways to our ruins."
I know not what to do; my wicked hopes
Are, with this tempest, torn up by the roots.
Oh, which way shall I bend my desperate steps,
In which unsufferable shame and misery
Will not attend them? I will walk this bank,
And see if I can meet the other relics
Of our poor shipwrack'd crew, or hear of them.
The knight, alas, was so far gone with wine,
And th' other three, that I refus'd their boat,
And took the hapless woman in another,
Who cannot but be sunk, whatever Fortune

Hath wrought upon the others' desperate lives.

Exit.

Enter PETRONEL and SEAGULL, bareheaded.

SIR PETRONEL - Zounds, Captain, I tell thee we are cast up o' the coast of France. 'S foot! I am not drunk still, I hope! Dost remember where we were last night?

SEAGULL - No, by my troth, knight, not I; but methinks we have been a horrible while upon the water and in the water.

SIR PETRONEL - Ay me, we are undone forever. Hast any money about thee?

SEAGULL - Not a penny, by Heaven!

SIR PETRONEL - Not a penny betwixt us, and cast ashore in France!

SEAGULL - Faith, I cannot tell that; my brains nor mine eyes are not mine own yet.

Enter two GENTLEMEN.

SIR PETRONEL - 'Sfoot! wilt not believe me? I know 't by th' elevation of the pole, and by the altitude and latitude of the climate. See! Here comes a couple of French gentlemen; I knew we were in France; dost thou think our Englishmen are so Frenchified that a man knows not whether he be in France or in England, when he sees 'em? What shall we do? We must e'en to 'em, and entreat some relief of 'em. Life is sweet, and we have no other means to relieve our lives now but their charities.

SEAGULL - Pray you, do you beg on 'em then; you can speak French.

SIR PETRONEL - Monsieur, plaist il d'avoir pitie de nostre grande infortunes? Je suis un povre chevalier d'Angleterre qui a souffri l'infortune de naufrage.

1ST GENTLEMAN - Un povre chevalier d'Angleterre?

SIR PETRONEL - Oui, monsieur, il est trop vraye; mais vous scaves bien nous sommes toutes subject a fortune.

2ND GENTLEMAN - A poor knight of England? — a poor knight of Windsor, are you not? Why speak you this broken French, when y' are a whole Englishman? On what coast are you, think you?

SIR PETRONEL - On the coast of France, sir.

1ST GENTLEMAN - On the coast of Dogs, sir; y' are i' th' Isle a' Dogs, I tell you. I see y' ave been wash'd in the Thames here, and I believe ye were drown'd in a tavern before, or else you would never have took boat in such a dawning as this was. Farewell, farewell; we will not know you, for shaming of you. — I ken the man weel; he's one of my thirty pound knights.

2ND GENTLEMAN - No, no, this is he that stole his knighthood o' the grand day for four pound, giving to a page all the money in's purse, I wot well.

Exeunt GENTLEMEN.

SEAGULL - Death! Colonel, I knew you were overshot.

SIR PETRONEL - Sure I think now, indeed, Captain Seagull, we were something overshot.

Enter QUICKSILVER.

What! my sweet Frank Quicksilver! dost thou survive, to rejoice me? But what! nobody at thy heels, Frank? Ay me! what is become of poor Mistress Security?

QUICKSILVER - Faith, gone quite from her name, as she is from her fame, I think; I left her to the mercy of the water.

SEAGULL - Let her go, let her go! Let us go to our ship at Blackwall, and shift us.

SIR PETRONEL - Nay, by my troth, let our clothes rot upon us, and let us rot in them; twenty to one our ship is attach'd by this time! If we set her not under sail this last tide, I never look'd for any other. Woe, woe is me! what shall become of us? The last money we could make the greedy Thames has devour'd; and, if our ship be attach'd, there is no hope can relieve us.

QUICKSILVER - 'Sfoot, knight! what an unknightly faintness transports thee! Let our ship sink, and all the world that's without us be taken from us, I hope I have some tricks in this brain of mine shall not let us perish.

SEAGULL - Well said, Frank, i' faith. O my nimble-spirited Quicksilver! 'Fore God, would thou hadst been our colonel!

SIR PETRONEL - I like his spirit rarely; but I see no means he has to support that spirit.

QUICKSILVER - Go to, knight! I have more means than thou art aware of. I have not liv'd amongst goldsmiths and goldmakers all this while but I have learned something worthy of my time with 'em. And, not to let thee stink where thou stand'st, knight, I'll let thee know some of my skill presently.

SEAGULL - Do, good Frank, I beseech thee.

QUICKSILVER - I will blanch copper so cunningly that it shall endure all proofs but the test: it shall endure malleation, it shall have the ponderosity of Luna, and the tenacity of Luna, by no means friable.

SIR PETRONEL - 'Slight! where learn'st thou these terms, trow?

QUICKSILVER - Tush, knight! the terms of this art every ignorant quacksalver is perfect in; but I'll tell you how yourself shall blanch copper thus cunningly. Take ars'nic, otherwise call realga (which indeed is plain ratsbane); sublime him three or four times; then take the sublimate of this realga and put him into a glass, into chymia, and let him have a convenient decoction natural, four-and-twenty hours, and he will become perfectly fix'd; then take this fixed powder, and project him upon well-purg'd copper, et habebis magisterium.

OMNES - Excellent Frank, let us hug thee!

QUICKSILVER - Nay, this I will do besides: I'll take you off twelvepence from every angel, with a kind of aqua fortis, and never deface any part of the image.

SIR PETRONEL - But then it will want weight!

QUICKSILVER - You shall restore that thus: take your sal achyme prepar'd, and your distill'd urine, and let your angels lie in it but four-and-twenty hours, and they shall have their perfect weight again. Come on, now; I hope this is enough to put some spirit into the livers of you; I'll infuse more another time. We have saluted the proud air long enough with our bare sconces. Now will I have you to a wench's house of mine at London, there make shift to shift us, and, after, take such fortunes as the stars shall assign us.

OMNES - Notable Frank, we will ever adore thee!

Exeunt all but SLITGUT.

Enter DRAWER with WINIFRED new attir'd.

WINIFRED - Now, sweet friend, you have brought me near enough your tavern, which I desired that I might with some color be seen near, inquiring for my husband, who, I must tell you, stale thither last night with my wet gown we have left at your friend's, which, to continue your former honest kindness, let me pray you to keep close from the knowledge of any; and so, with all vow of your requital, let me now entreat you to leave me to my woman's wit, and fortune.

DRAWER - All shall be done you desire; and so all the fortune you can wish for attend you.

Exit DRAWER.

Enter SECURITY.

SECURITY - I will once more to this unhappy tavern before I shift one rag of me more; that I may there know what is left behind, and what news of their passengers. I have bought me a hat and band with the little money I had about me, and made the streets a little leave staring at my nightcap.

WINIFRED - Oh, my dear husband! where have you been to-night? All night abroad at taverns? Rob me of my garments, and fare as one run away from me? Alas! is this seemly for a man of your credit, of your age, and affection to your wife?

SECURITY - What should I say? how miraculously sorts this! Was not I at home, and call'd thee last night?

WINIFRED - Yes, sir, the harmless sleep you broke; and my answer to you would have witness'd it, if you had had the patience to have stay'd and answered me; but your so sudden retreat made me imagine you were gone to Master Bramble's, and so rested patient and hopeful of your coming again, till this your unbelieved absence brought me abroad with no less than wonder, to seek you where the false knight had carried you.

SECURITY - Villain and monster that I was! How have I abus'd thee! I was suddenly gone indeed, for my sudden jealousy transferred me! I will say no more but this, dear wife: I suspected thee.

WINIFRED - Did you suspect me?

SECURITY - Talk not of it, I beseech thee; I am ashamed to imagine it. I will home, I will home; and every morning on my knees ask thee heartily forgiveness.

Exeunt SECURITY and WINIFRED.

SLITGUT - Now will I descend my honorable prospect, the farthest-seeing sea-mark of the world: no marvel, then, if I could see two miles about me. I hope the red tempest's anger be now overblown, which sure I think Heaven sent as a punishment for profaning holy Saint Luke's memory with so ridiculous a custom. Thou dishonest satire! Farewell to honest married men! farewell to all sorts and degrees of thee! Farewell, thou horn of hunger, that call'st th' inns a' court to their manger! Farewell, thou horn of abundance, that adornest the headsmen of the commonwealth! Farewell, thou horn of direction, that is the city lanthorn! Farewell, thou horn of pleasure, the ensign of the huntsman! Farewell, thou horn of destiny, th' ensign of the married man! Farewell, thou horn tree, that bearest nothing but stone fruit!

Exit.

SCENE II - A ROOM IN TOUCHSTONE'S HOUSE

TOUCHSTONE - Ha, sirrah! thinks my knight adventurer we can no point of our compass? Do we not know north-north-east, north-east and by east, east and by north, nor plain eastward? Ha! have we never heard of Virginia, nor the Cavallaria, nor the Colonoria? Can we discover no discoveries? Well, mine errant Sir Flash, and my runagate Quicksilver, you may drink drunk, crack cans, hurl away a brown dozen of Monmouth caps or so, in sea-ceremony to your bon voyage; but, for reaching any coast, save the coast of Kent or Essex, with this tide, or with this fleet, I'll be your warrant for a Gravesend toast. There's that gone afore will stay your admiral and vice-admiral and rear-admiral, were they all (as they are) but one pinnace, and under sail, as well as a remora, doubt it not; and from this sconce, without either powder or shot. Work upon that now! Nay, an you'll show tricks, we'll vie with you a little. My daughter, his lady, was sent eastward by land to a castle of his i' the air, in what region I know not, and, as I hear, was glad to take up her lodging in her coach, she and her two waiting women (her maid, and her mother), like three snails in a shell, and the coachman a-top on 'em, I think. Since, they have all found the way back again by Weeping Cross; but I'll not see 'em. And, for two on 'em, madam and her malkin, they are like to bite o' the bridle for William, as the poor horses have done all this while that hurried 'em, or else go graze o' the common. So should my Dame Touchstone too; but she has been my cross these thirty years, and I'll now keep her to fright away sprites, i' faith. I wonder I hear no news of my son Golding! He was sent for to the Guildhall this morning betimes, and I marvel at the matter; if I had not laid up comfort and hope in him, I should grow desperate of all. See, he is come i' my thought! —

Enter GOLDING.

How now, son? What news at the Court of Aldermen?

GOLDING - Troth, sir, an accident somewhat strange; else, it hath little in it worth the reporting.

TOUCHSTONE - What? It is not borrowing of money, then?

GOLDING - No, sir; it hath pleas'd the worshipful Commoners of the city to take me one i' their number at presentation of the inquest ——

TOUCHSTONE - Ha!

GOLDING - And the alderman of the ward wherein I dwell to appoint me his deputy ——

TOUCHSTONE - How?

GOLDING - In which place I have had an oath minist'red me, since I went.

TOUCHSTONE - Now, my dear and happy son, let me kiss thy new Worship, and a little boast mine own happiness in thee. — What a fortune was it (or rather my judgment, indeed) for me first to see that in his disposition which a whole city so conspires to second! Ta'en into the livery of his company the first day of his freedom! Now, not a week married, chosen Commoner and alderman's deputy in a day! Note but the reward of a thrifty course. The wonder of his time! Well, I will honor Master Alderman for this act, as becomes me, and shall think the better of the Common Council's wisdom and worship, while I live, for thus meeting, or but coming after me, in the opinion of his desert. Forward, my sufficient son! and, as this is the first, so esteem it the least step to that high and prime honor that expects thee.

GOLDING - Sir, as I was not ambitious of this, so I covet no higher place; it hath dignity enough, if it will but save me from contempt; and I had rather my bearing in this or any other office should add worth to it than the place give the least opinion to me.

TOUCHSTONE - Excellently spoken! This modest answer of thine blushes, as if it said, "I will wear scarlet shortly." Worshipful son! I cannot contain myself; I must tell thee, I hope to see thee one o' the monuments of our city, and reckon'd among her worthies, to be rememb'red the same day with the Lady Ramsey and grave Gresham, when the famous fable of Whittington and his puss shall be forgotten, and thou and thy acts become the posies for hospitals; when thy name shall be written upon conduits, and thy deeds play'd i' thy lifetime by the best companies of actors, and be call'd their get-penny. This I divine; this I prophesy.

GOLDING - Sir, engage not your expectation farder than my abilities will answer; I, that know mine own strengths, fear 'em; and there is so seldom a loss in promising the least that commonly it brings with it a welcome deceit. I have other news for you, sir.

TOUCHSTONE - None more welcome, I am sure.

GOLDING - They have their degree of welcome, I dare affirm. The colonel and all his company, this morning putting forth drunk from Billingsgate, had like to have been cast away o' this side Greenwich; and, as I have intelligence by a false brother, are come dropping to town like so many masterless men, i' their doublets and hose, without hat or cloak or any other —

TOUCHSTONE - A miracle! the justice of Heaven! Where are they? Let's go presently and lay for 'em.

GOLDING - I have done that already, sir, both by constables and other officers, who shall take 'em at their old Anchor, and with less tumult or suspicion than if yourself were seen in 't, under color of a great press that is now abroad; and they shall here be brought afore me.

TOUCHSTONE - Prudent and politic son! Disgrace 'em all that ever thou canst; their ship I have already arrested. How to my wish it falls out that thou hast the place of a justicer upon 'em! I am partly glad of the injury done to me, that thou mayst punish it. Be severe i' thy place, like a new officer o' the first quarter, unreflected. You hear how our lady is come back with her train from the invisible castle?

GOLDING - No; where is she?

TOUCHSTONE - Within; but I ha' not seen her yet, nor her mother, who now begins to wish her daughter undubb'd, they say, and that she had walk'd a foot-pace with her sister. Here they come; stand back.

Enter MISTRESS TOUCHSTONE, GERTRUDE, MILDRED, and SINDEFY.

God save your Ladyship; 'save your good Ladyship! Your Ladyship is welcome from your enchanted castle; so are your beauteous retinue. I hear your knight errant is travell'd on strange adventures. Surely, in my mind, your Ladyship hath "fish'd fair, and caught a frog," as the saying is.

MISTRESS TOUCHSTONE - Speak to your father, madam, and kneel down.

GERTRUDE - Kneel? I hope I am not brought so low yet; though my knight be run away, and has sold my land, I am a lady still.

TOUCHSTONE - Your Ladyship says true, madam; and it is fitter and a greater decorum that I should curtsy to you that are a knight's wife and a lady than you be brought a' your knees to me, who am a poor cullion and your father.

GERTRUDE - Law! my father knows his duty.

MISTRESS TOUCHSTONE - Oh, child!

TOUCHSTONE - And therefore I do desire your Ladyship, my good Lady Flash, in all humility, to depart my obscure cottage, and return in quest of your bright and most transparent castle, "how ever presently conceal'd to mortal eyes." And, as for one poor woman of your train here, I will take that order she shall no longer be a charge unto you, nor help to spend your Ladyship; she shall stay at home with me, and not go abroad, not put you to the pawning of an odd coach horse or three wheels, but take part with the Touchstone. If we lack, we will not complain to your Ladyship. And so, good madam, with your damosel here, please you to let us see your straight backs in equipage; for truly here is no roost for such chickens as you are, or birds o' your feather, if it like your Ladyship.

GERTRUDE - Marry, fyste o' your kindness! I thought as much. Come away, Sin; we shall "as soon get a fart from a dead man as a farthing" of court'sy here.

MILDRED - Oh, good Sister!

GERTRUDE - Sister, Sir Reverence! Come away, I say; hunger drops out at his nose.

GOLDING - Oh, madam, "Fair words never hurt the tongue."

GERTRUDE - How say you by that? You come out with your gold-ends now!

MISTRESS TOUCHSTONE - Stay, Lady-daughter. Good husband —

TOUCHSTONE - Wife, "no man loves his fetters, be they made of gold." I list not "ha' my head fast'ned under my child's girdle;" "as she has brew'd, so let her drink," a' God's name. She "went witless to wedding," now she may "go wisely a-begging." It's but honeymoon yet with her Ladyship; she has coach horses, apparel, jewels yet left; she needs care for no friends, nor take knowledge of father, mother, brother, sister, or anybody. When those are pawn'd or spent, perhaps we shall return into the list of her acquaintance.

GERTRUDE - I scorn it, i' faith. — Come, Sin.

MISTRESS TOUCHSTONE - Oh, madam, why do you provoke your father thus?

Exit GERTRUDE with SINDEFY.

TOUCHSTONE - Nay, nay, e'en "let pride go afore; shame will follow after," I warrant you. Come, why dost thou weep now? Thou art not "the first good cow" hast "had an ill calf," I trust. —

[Exit MISTRESS TOUCHSTONE.]

What's the news with that fellow?

Enter CONSTABLE.

GOLDING - Sir, the knight and your man Quicksilver are without; will you ha' 'em brought in?

TOUCHSTONE - Oh, by any means. [Exit Constable.] And, son, here's a chair; appear terrible unto 'em on the first interview. Let them behold the melancholy of a magistrate, and taste the fury of a citizen in office.

GOLDING - Why, sir, I can do nothing to 'em, except you charge 'em with somewhat.
TOUCHSTONE - I will charge 'em and recharge 'em, rather than authority should want foil to set it off.

Offers GOLDING a chair.

GOLDING - No, good sir, I will not.

TOUCHSTONE - Son, it is your place; by any means —

GOLDING - Believe it, I will not, sir.

Enter KNIGHT PETRONEL, QUICKSILVER, CONSTABLE, and Officers.

SIR PETRONEL - How misfortune pursues us still in our misery!

QUICKSILVER - Would it had been my fortune to have been truss'd up at Wapping rather than ever ha' come here!

SIR PETRONEL - Or mine to have famish'd in the Island!

QUICKSILVER - Must Golding sit upon us?

CONSTABLE - You might carry a Master under your girdle to Master Deputy's Worship.

GOLDING - What are those, Master Constable?

CONSTABLE - An 't please your Worship, a couple of masterless men I press'd for the Low Countries, sir.

GOLDING - Why do you not carry 'em to Bridewell, according to your order, they may be shipp'd away?

CONSTABLE - An 't please your Worship, one of 'em says he is a knight; and we thought good to show him to your Worship, for our discharge.

GOLDING - Which is he?

CONSTABLE - This, sir.

GOLDING - And what's the other?

CONSTABLE - A knight's fellow, sir, an 't please you.

GOLDING - What! a knight and his fellow thus accout'red? Where are their hats and feathers, their rapiers and their cloaks?

QUICKSILVER - [aside] Oh, they mock us.

CONSTABLE - Nay, truly, sir, they had cast both their feathers and hats, too, before we see 'em. Here's all their furniture, an 't please you, that we found. They say knights are now to be known without feathers, like cock'rels by their spurs, sir.

GOLDING - What are their names, say they?

TOUCHSTONE - [aside] Very well, this. He should not take knowledge of 'em in his place, indeed.

CONSTABLE - This is Sir Petronel Flash.

TOUCHSTONE - How!

CONSTABLE - And this, Francis Quicksilver.

TOUCHSTONE - Is 't possible? I thought your Worship had been gone for Virginia, sir; you are welcome home, sir. Your Worship has made a quick return, it seems, and no doubt a good voyage. Nay, pray you be cover'd, sir. How did your biscuit hold out, sir? — Methought I had seen this gentleman afore. Good Master Quicksilver, how a degree to the southward has chang'd you!

GOLDING - Do you know 'em, Father? — Forbear your offers a little, you shall be heard anon.

TOUCHSTONE - Yes, Master Deputy; I had a small venture with them in the voyage — a thing call'd a son-in-law, or so. — Officers, you may let 'em stand alone: they will not run away; I'll give my word for them, a couple of very honest gentlemen. One of 'em was my prentice, Master Quicksilver here; and when he had two year to serve, kept his whore and his hunting nag, would play his hundred pound at gresco or primero as familiarly (and all a' my purse) as any bright piece of crimson on 'em all; had his changeable trunks of apparel standing at livery, with his mare, his chest of perfum'd linen, and his bathing-tubs, which, when I told him of, why he — he was a gentleman, and I a poor Cheapside groom! The remedy was, we must part. Since when he hath had the gift of gathering up some small parcels of mine, to the value of five hundred pound, dispers'd among my customers, to furnish this his Virginian venture; wherein this knight was the chief, Sir Flash — one that married a daughter of mine, ladified her, turned two thousand pounds' worth of good land of hers into cash within the first week, bought her a new gown and a coach; sent her to seek her fortune by land, whilst himself prepared for his fortune by sea; took in fresh flesh at Billingsgate, for his own diet, to serve him the whole voyage — the wife of a certain usurer call'd Security, who hath been the broker for 'em in all this business. Please, Master Deputy, work upon that now!

GOLDING - If my worshipful father have ended —

TOUCHSTONE - I have, it shall please Master Deputy.

GOLDING - Well then, under correction —

TOUCHSTONE - [aside] Now, son, come over 'em with some fine gird, as thus, "Knight, you shall be encount'red," that is, had to the Counter; or, "Quicksilver, I will put you in a crucible," or so.

GOLDING - Sir Petronel Flash, I am sorry to see such flashes as these proceed from a gentleman of your quality and rank; for mine own part, I could wish I could say I could not see them; but such is the misery of magistrates and men in place, that they must not wink at offenders. — Take him aside. — I will hear you anon, sir.

TOUCHSTONE - [aside] I like this well, yet; there's some grace i' the knight left: he cries.

GOLDING - Francis Quicksilver, would God thou hadst turn'd quacksalver, rather than run into these dissolute and lewd courses! It is great pity; thou art a proper young man, of an honest and clean face, somewhat near a good one; God hath done his part in thee; but thou hast made too much, and been too proud, of that face, with the rest of thy body; for maintenance of which in neat and garish attire, only to be look'd upon by some light housewives, thou hast prodigally consumed much of thy master's estate; and, being by him gently admonish'd at several times, hast return'd thyself haughty and rebellious in thine answers, thund'ring out uncivil comparisons, requiting all his kindness with a coarse and harsh behavior; never returning thanks for any one benefit, but receiving all as if they had been debts to thee, and no courtesies. I must tell thee, Francis, these are manifest signs of an ill nature; and God doth often punish such pride and outrecuidance with scorn and infamy, which is the worst of misfortune. — My worshipful father, what do you please to charge them withal? — From the press I will free 'em, Master Constable.

CONSTABLE - Then I'll leave your Worship, sir.

GOLDING - No, you may stay; there will be other matters against 'em.

TOUCHSTONE - Sir, I do charge this gallant, Master Quicksilver, on suspicion of felony; and the knight, as being accessary in the receipt of my goods.

QUICKSILVER - O God, sir!

TOUCHSTONE - Hold thy peace, impudent varlet, hold thy peace! With what forehead or face dost thou offer to chop logic with me, having run such a race of riot as thou hast done? Does not the sight of this worshipful man's fortune and temper confound thee, that was thy younger fellow in household, and now come to have the place of a judge upon thee? Dost not observe this? Which of all thy gallants and gamesters, thy swearers and thy swaggerers, will come now to moan thy misfortune, or pity thy penury? They'll look out at a window, as thou rid'st in triumph to Tyburn, and cry, "Yonder goes honest Frank, mad Quicksilver!" "He was a free boon companion, when he had money," says one. "Hang him, fool;" says another; "he could not keep it when he had it!" "A pox o' the cullion, his master," says a third; "he has brought him to this;" when their pox of pleasure, and their piles of perdition, would have been better bestowed upon thee, that hast vent'red for 'em with the best, and by the clue of thy knavery brought thyself weeping to the cart of calamity.

QUICKSILVER - Worshipful Master!

TOUCHSTONE - Offer not to speak, crocodile; I will not hear a sound come from thee. Thou hast learn'd to whine at the play yonder. — Master Deputy, pray you commit 'em both to safe custody, till I be able farther to charge 'em.

QUICKSILVER - O me! what an infortunate thing am I!

SIR PETRONEL - Will you not take security, sir?

TOUCHSTONE - Yes, marry, will I, Sir Flash, if I can find him, and charge him as deep as the best on you. He has been the plotter of all this; he is your enginer, I hear. Master Deputy, you'll dispose of these? In the mean time, I'll to my Lord Mayor, and get his warrant to seize that serpent, Security, into my hands, and seal up both house and goods to the King's use or my satisfaction.

GOLDING - Officers, take 'em to the Counter.

QUICKSILVER and SIR PETRONEL - O God!

TOUCHSTONE - Nay, on, on; you see the issue of your sloth. Of sloth cometh pleasure, of pleasure cometh riot, of riot comes whoring, of whoring comes spending, of spending comes want, of want comes theft, of theft comes hanging; and there is my Quicksilver fix'd.

Exeunt.

ACT V — SCENE I – AN ALEHOUSE

Enter GERTRUDE and SINDEFY.

GERTRUDE - Ah, Sin! hast thou ever read i' the chronicle of any lady and her waiting woman driven to that extremity that we are, Sin?

SINDEFY - Not I, truly, madam; and, if I had, it were but cold comfort should come out of books, now.

GERTRUDE - Why, good faith, Sin, I could dine with a lamentable story, now. O hone, hone, o no nera! etc. Canst thou tell ne'er a one, Sin?

SINDEFY - None but mine own, madam, which is lamentable enough: first to be stol'n from my friends, which were worshipful and of good account, by a prentice in the habit and disguise of a gentleman, and here brought up to London, and promis'd marriage, and now likely to be forsaken, for he is in possibility to be hang'd!

GERTRUDE - Nay, weep not, good Sin; my Petronel is in as good possibility as he. Thy miseries are nothing to mine, Sin; I was more than promis'd marriage, Sin; I had it, Sin; and was made a lady; and by a knight, Sin; which is now as good as no knight, Sindefy. And I was born in London, which is more then brought up, Sin; and already forsaken, which is past likelihood, Sin; and, instead of land i' the country, all my knight's living lies i' the Counter, Sin; there's his castle, now!

SINDEFY - Which he cannot be forc'd out of, madam.

GERTRUDE - Yes, if he would live hungry a week or two. "Hunger," they say, "breaks stone walls." But he is e'en well enough serv'd, Sin, that, so soon as ever he had got my hand to the sale of my inheritance, run away from me, as I had been his punk, God bless us! Would the Knight o' the Sun or Palmerin of England, have us'd their ladies so, Sin? or Sir Lancelot or Sir Tristram?

SINDEFY - I do not know, madam.

GERTRUDE - Then thou know'st nothing, Sindefy. Thou art a fool, Sindefy. The knighthood nowadays are nothing like the knighthood of old time. They rid a-horseback; ours go afoot. They were attended by their squires, ours by their lackeys. They went buckled in their armor, ours muffled in their cloaks. They travell'd wildernesses and deserts; ours dare scarce walk the streets. They were still press'd to engage their honor, ours still ready to pawn their clothes. They would gallop on at sight of a monster; ours run away at sight of a sergeant. They would help poor ladies; ours make poor ladies.

SINDEFY - Ay, madam, they were knights of the Round Table at Winchester, that sought adventures; but these, of the Square Table at ordinaries, that sit at hazard.

GERTRUDE - True, Sin; let him vanish. And tell me, what shall we pawn next?

SINDEFY - Ay, marry, madam, a timely consideration; for our hostess, profane woman, has sworn by bread and salt she will not trust us another meal.

GERTRUDE - Let it stink in her hand then. I'll not be beholding to her. Let me see; my jewels be gone, and my gowns, and my red velvet petticoat that I was married in, and my wedding silk stockings, and all thy best apparel, poor Sin! Good faith, rather than thou shouldest pawn a rag more I'd lay my ladyship in lavender — if I knew where.

SINDEFY - Alas, madam, your ladyship?

GERTRUDE - Ay. Why? You do not scorn my ladyship, though it is in a waistcoat? God's my life! you are a peat indeed! Do I offer to mortgage my ladyship for you and for your avail, and do you turn the lip and the "alas!" to my ladyship?

SINDEFY - No, madam; but I make question who will lend anything upon it.

GERTRUDE - Who? marry, enow, I warrant you, if you'll seek 'em out. I'm sure I remember the time when I would ha' given a thousand pound, if I had it, to have been a lady; and I hope I was not bred and born with that appetite alone; some other gentle-born o' the city have the same longing, I trust. And, for my part, I would afford 'em a penny'rth; my ladyship is little the worse for the wearing, and yet I would bate a good deal of the sum. I would lend it, let me see, for forty pounds in hand, Sin; that would apparel us; and ten pound a year: that would keep me and you, Sin, with our needles; and we should never need to be beholding to our scurvy parents! Good Lord! that there are no fairies nowadays, Sin.

SINDEFY - Why, madam?

GERTRUDE - To do miracles, and bring ladies money. Sure, if we lay in a cleanly house, they would haunt it, Sin! I'll try. I'll sweep the chamber soon at night, and set a dish of water o' the hearth. A fairy may come and bring a pearl, or a diamond. We do not know, SINDEFY - Or there may be a pot of gold hid o' the back-side, if we had tools to dig for 't! Why may not we two rise early i' the morning, Sin, afore anybody is up, and find a jewel i' the streets worth a hundred pound? May not some great court-lady, as she comes from revels at midnight, look out of her coach as 't is running, and lose such a jewel, and we find it? Ha?

SINDEFY - They are pretty waking dreams, these.

GERTRUDE - Or may not some old usurer be drunk overnight, with a bag of money, and leave it behind him on a stall? For God-sake, Sin, let's rise to-morrow by break of day and see. I protest, law, if I had as much money as an alderman, I would scatter some on 't i' th' streets for poor ladies to find, when their knights were laid up. And, now I remember my song o' the "Golden Show'r": why may not I have such fortune? I'll sing it, and try what luck I shall have after it.

Fond fables tell of old
How Jove in Danaë's lap
Fell in a shower of gold,
By which she caught a clap;
Oh, had it been my hap,
(Howe'er the blow doth threaten)
So well I like the play,
That I could wish all day
And night to be so beaten.

Enter MISTRESS TOUCHSTONE.

Oh, here's my mother! Good luck, I hope. — Ha' you brought any money, Mother? Pray you, Mother, your blessing. Nay, sweet Mother, do not weep.

MISTRESS TOUCHSTONE - God bless you! I would I were in my grave!

GERTRUDE - Nay, dear Mother, can you steal no more money from my father? Dry your eyes, and comfort me. Alas! it is my knight's fault, and not mine, that I am in a waistcoat, and attired thus simply.

MISTRESS TOUCHSTONE - Simply? 'T is better than thou deserv'st. Never whimper for the matter. "Thou should'st have look'd before thou hadst leap'd." Thou wert afire to be a lady, and now your ladyship and you may both "blow at the coal," for aught I know. "Self do, self have." "The hasty person never wants woe," they say.

GERTRUDE - Nay then, Mother, you should ha' look'd to it. A body would think you were the older! I did but my kind, I. He was a knight, and I was fit to be a lady. 'T is not lack of liking, but lack of living, that severs us. And you talk like yourself and a citiner in this, i' faith. You show what husband you come on, iwis. You smell the Touchstone — he that will do more for his daughter that he has married to a scurvy gold-end man and his prentice, than he will for his tother daughter, that has wedded a knight and his customer. By this light, I think he is not my legitimate father.

SINDEFY - Oh, good madam, do not take up your mother so!

MISTRESS TOUCHSTONE - Nay, nay, let her e'en alone. Let her Ladyship grieve me still, with her bitter taunts and terms. I have not dole enough to see her in this miserable case, ay, without her velvet gowns, without ribands, without jewels, without French wires, or cheat bread, or quails, or a little dog, or a gentleman usher, or anything, indeed, that's fit for a lady —

SINDEFY - [aside] Except her tongue.

MISTRESS TOUCHSTONE - And I not able to relieve her, neither, being kept so short by my husband. Well, God knows my heart. I did little think that ever she should have need of her sister Golding!

GERTRUDE - Why Mother, I ha' not yet. Alas! good Mother, be not intoxicate for me; I am well enough; I would not change husbands with my sister, I. "The leg of a lark is better than the body of a kite."

MISTRESS TOUCHSTONE - I know that; but —

GERTRUDE - What, sweet Mother, what?

MISTRESS TOUCHSTONE - It's but ill food, when nothing's left but the claw.

GERTRUDE - That's true, Mother. Ay me!

MISTRESS TOUCHSTONE - Nay, sweet ladybird, sigh not. Child, madam; why do you weep thus? Be of good cheer; I shall die if you cry, and mar your complexion thus.

GERTRUDE - Alas, Mother, what should I do?

MISTRESS TOUCHSTONE - Go to thy sister's, child; she'll be proud thy Ladyship will come under her roof. She'll win thy father to release thy knight, and redeem thy gowns and thy coach and thy horses, and set thee up again.

GERTRUDE - But will she get him to set my knight up too?

MISTRESS TOUCHSTONE - That she will, or anything else thou'lt ask her.

GERTRUDE - I will begin to love her, if I thought she would do this.

MISTRESS TOUCHSTONE - Try her, good chuck; I warrant thee.

GERTRUDE - Dost thou think she'll do 't?

SINDEFY - Ay, madam, and be glad you will receive it.

MISTRESS TOUCHSTONE - That's a good maiden; she tells you true. Come, I'll take order for your debts i' the alehouse.

Exeunt.

GERTRUDE - Go, Sin, and pray for thy Frank, as I will for my Pet.

SCENE II

Enter TOUCHSTONE, GOLDING, and WOLF.

TOUCHSTONE - I will receive no letters, Master Wolf; you shall pardon me.

GOLDING - Good Father, let me entreat you.

TOUCHSTONE - Son Golding, I will not be tempted; I find mine own easy nature, and I know not what a well-penn'd, subtle letter may work upon it; there may be tricks, packing, do you see? Return with your packet, sir.

WOLF - Believe it, sir, you need fear no packing here; these are but letters of submission, all.

TOUCHSTONE - Sir, I do look for no submission. I will bear myself in this like blind Justice. Work upon that now! When the sessions come, they shall hear from me.

GOLDING - From whom come your letters, Master Wolf?

WOLF - An 't please you, sir, one from Sir Petronel, another from Francis Quicksilver, and a third from old Security, who is almost mad in prison. There are two to your Worship; one from Master Francis, sir; another from the knight.

TOUCHSTONE - I do wonder, Master Wolf, why you should travail thus, in a business so contrary to kind or the nature o' your place; that you, being the keeper of a prison, should labor the release of your prisoners; whereas, methinks, it were far more natural and kindly in you to be ranging about for more, and not let these scape you have already under the tooth. But they say you wolves, when you ha' suck'd the blood, once that they are dry, you ha' done.

WOLF - Sir, your Worship may descant as you please o' my name; but I protest I was never so mortified with any men's discourse or behavior in prison; yet I have had of all sorts of men i' the kingdom under my keys; and almost of all religions i' the land, as Papist, Protestant, Puritan, Brownist, Anabaptist, Millenary, Family o' Love, Jew, Turk, Infidel, Atheist, Good Fellow, etc.

GOLDING - And which of all these, thinks Master Wolf, was the best religion?

WOLF - Troth, Master Deputy, they that pay fees best; we never examine their consciences farder.

GOLDING - I believe you, Master Wolf— Good faith, sir, here's a great deal of humility i' these letters!

WOLF - Humility, sir? Ay. Were your Worship an eyewitness of it, you would say so. The knight will i' the Knights' Ward, do what we can, sir; and Master Quicksilver would be i' the Hole, if we would let him. I never knew or saw prisoners more penitent or more devout. They will sit you up all night singing of psalms, and edifying the whole prison; only Security sings a note too high sometimes, because he lies i' the Twopenny Ward, far off, and cannot take his tune. The neighbors can not rest for him, but come every morning to ask what godly prisoners we have.

TOUCHSTONE - Which on 'em is 't is so devout, the knight or the tother?

WOLF - Both, sir; but the young man especially. I never heard his like. He has cut his hair too. He is so well given, and has such good gifts. He can tell you almost all the stories of the Book of Martyrs, and speak you all the Sick Man's Salve without book.

TOUCHSTONE - Ay, if he had had grace, he was brought up where it grew, iwis. — On, Master Wolf.

WOLF - And he has converted one Fangs, a sergeant, a fellow could neither write nor read; he was called the Bandog o' the Counter; and he has brought him already to pare his nails and say his prayers; and 't is hop'd, he will sell his place shortly, and become an intelligencer.

TOUCHSTONE - No more; I am coming already. If I should give any farther ear, I were taken. Adieu, good Master Wolf—Son, I do feel mine own weaknesses; do not importune me. Pity is a rheum that I am subject to; but I will resist it. Master Wolf, "Fish is cast away that is cast in dry pools." Tell Hypocrisy it will not do; I have touch'd and tried too often; I am yet proof, and I will remain so. When the sessions come, they shall hear from me. In the meantime, to all suits, to all entreaties, to all letters, to all tricks, I will be deaf as an adder and blind as a beetle, lay mine ear to the ground, and lock mine eyes i' my hand against all temptations.

Exit.

GOLDING - You see, Master Wolf, how inexorable he is. There is no hope to recover him. Pray you commend me to my brother knight, and to my fellow Francis [giving money]; present 'em with this small token of my love; tell 'em, I wish I could do 'em any worthier office; but, in this, 't is desperate: yet I will not fail to try the uttermost of my power for 'em. And, sir, as far as I have any credit with you, pray you let 'em want nothing; though I am not ambitious they should know so much.

WOLF - Sir, both your actions and words speak you to be a true gentleman. They shall know only what is fit, and no more.

Exeunt.

SCENE III – A ROOM IN THE COUNTER

Enter HOLDFAST and BRAMBLE.

HOLDFAST - Who would you speak with, sir?

BRAMBLE - I would speak with one Security, that is prisoner here.

HOLDFAST - You are welcome, sir. Stay there, I'll call him to you. — Master Security!

SECURITY appears at a grating.

SECURITY - Who calls?

HOLDFAST - Here's a gentleman would speak with you.

SECURITY - What is he? Is 't one that grafts my forehead now I am in prison, and comes to see how the horns shoot up and prosper?

HOLDFAST - You must pardon him, sir; the old man is a little craz'd with his imprisonment.

Exit.

SECURITY - What say you to me, sir? Look you here, my learned counsel, Master Bramble! Cry you mercy, sir! When saw you my wife?

BRAMBLE - She is now at my house, sir; and desir'd me that I would come to visit you, and inquire of you your case, that we might work some means to get you forth.

SECURITY - My case, Master Bramble, is stone walls and iron grates; you see it; this is the weakest part on 't. And, for getting me forth, no means but hang myself, and so to be carried forth, from which they have here bound me in intolerable bands.

BRAMBLE - Why, but what is 't you are in for, sir?

SECURITY - For my sins, for my sins, sir, whereof marriage is the greatest. Oh, had I never married, I had never know this purgatory, to which hell is a kind of cool bath in respect; my wife's confederacy, sir, with old Touchstone, that she might keep her jubilee and the feast of her new moon. Do you understand me, sir?

Enter QUICKSILVER.

QUICKSILVER - Good sir, go in and talk with him. The light does him harm, and his example will be hurtful to the weak prisoners. — Fie, Father Security, that you'll be still so profane! Will nothing humble you?

Exeunt SECURITY, BRAMBLE, and QUICKSILVER.

Enter two PRISONERS, with a FRIEND.

FRIEND - What's he?

1ST PRISONER - Oh, he is a rare young man! Do you not know him?

FRIEND - Not I. I never saw him I can remember.

2ND PRISONER - Why, it is he that was the gallant prentice of London — Master Touchstone's man.

FRIEND - Who? Quicksilver?

1ST PRISONER - Ay, this is he.

FRIEND - Is this he? They say he has been a gallant indeed.

2ND PRISONER - Oh, the royallest fellow that ever was bred up i' the city. He would play you his thousand pound a night at dice; keep knights and lords company; go with them to bawdyhouses; had his six men in a livery; kept a stable of hunting horses, and his wench in her velvet gown and her cloth of silver. Here's one knight with him here in prison.

FRIEND - And how miserably he is chang'd!

1ST PRISONER - Oh, that's voluntary in him; he gave away all his rich clothes, as soon as ever he came in here, among the prisoners; and will eat o' the basket, for humility.

FRIEND - Why will he do so?

1ST PRISONER - Alas, he has no hope of life! He mortifies himself. He does but linger on till the sessions.

2ND PRISONER - O, he has penn'd the best thing, that he calls his "Repentance" or his "Last Farewell," that ever you heard. He is a pretty poet; and, for prose — you would wonder how many prisoners he has help'd out, with penning petitions for 'em, and not take a penny. Look! this is the knight, in the rug-gown. Stand by.

Enter PETRONEL, BRAMBLE, and QUICKSILVER.

BRAMBLE - Sir, for Security's case, I have told him: say he should be condemned to be carted or whipp'd for a bawd, or so, why, I'll lay an execution on him o' two hundred pound; let him acknowledge a judgment, he shall do it in half an hour; they shall not all fetch him out without paying the execution, o' my word.

SIR PETRONEL - But can we not be bail'd, Master Bramble?

BRAMBLE - Hardly; there are none of the judges in town, else you should remove yourself, in spite of him, with a habeas corpus. But, if you have a friend to deliver your tale sensibly to some justice o' the town, that he may have feeling of it, do you see, you may be bail'd; for, as I understand the case, 't is only done in terrorem; and you shall have an action of false imprisonment against him when you come out, and perhaps a thousand pound costs.

Enter MASTER WOLF.

QUICKSILVER - How now, Master Wolf? what news? what return?
WOLF - Faith, bad all: yonder will be no letters received. He says the sessions shall determine it. Only Master Deputy Golding commends him to you, and, with this token, wishes he could do you other good.

Gives money.

QUICKSILVER - I thank him. — Good Master Bramble, trouble our quiet no more; do not molest us in prison thus with your winding devices; pray you depart. [Exit BRAMBLE.] — For my part, I commit my cause to Him that can succor me; let God work his will. Master Wolf, I pray you let this be distributed among the prisoners, and desire 'em to pray for us.

Exit QUICKSILVER.

WOLF - It shall be done, Master Frances.

1ST PRISONER - An excellent temper!

2ND PRISONER - Now God send him good luck.

Exeunt two PRISONERS and Friend.

SIR PETRONEL - But what said my father-in-law, Master Wolf?

Re-enter HOLDFAST.

HOLDFAST - Here's one would speak with you, sir.

WOLF - I'll tell you anon, Sir Petronel.

[Exit PETRONEL.]

— Who is 't?

HOLDFAST - A gentleman, sir, that will not be seen.

WOLF - Where is he?

Enter GOLDING.

Master Deputy! your Worship is welcome —

GOLDING - Peace!

Exit HOLDFAST.

WOLF - Away, sirrah!

GOLDING - Good faith, Master Wolf, the estate of these gentlemen, for whom you were so late and willing a suitor, doth much affect me; and, because I am desirous to do them some fair office, and find there is no means to make my father relent so likely as to bring him to be a spectator of their miseries, I have ventur'd on a device; which is to make myself your prisoner, entreating you will presently go report it to my father, and feigning an action, at suit of some third person, pray him, by this token, [giving a ring] that he will presently, and with all secrecy, come hither for my bail; which train, if any, I know will bring him abroad; and then, having him here, I doubt not but we shall be all fortunate in the event.

WOLF - Sir, I will put on my best speed to effect it. Please you come in.

GOLDING - Yes; and let me rest conceal'd, I pray you.

WOLF - See here a benefit truly done, when it is done timely, freely, and to no ambition.

Exeunt.

Enter TOUCHSTONE, Wife, Daughters, SINDEFY, and WINIFRED.

TOUCHSTONE - I will sail by you, and not hear you, like the wise Ulysses.

MILDRED - Dear Father!

MISTRESS TOUCHSTONE - Husband!

GERTRUDE - Father!

WINIFRED and SINDEFY - Master Touchstone!

TOUCHSTONE - Away, sirens, I will inmure myself against your cries, and lock myself up to your lamentations.

MISTRESS TOUCHSTONE - Gentle husband, hear me!

GERTRUDE - Father, it is I, Father, my Lady Flash. My sister and I am friends.

MILDRED - Good Father!

WINIFRED - Be not hard'ned, good Master Touchstone!

SINDEFY - I pray you, sir, be merciful!

TOUCHSTONE - I am deaf; I do not hear you; I have stopp'd mine ears with shoemakers' wax, and drunk Lethe and mandragora, to forget you. All you speak to me I commit to the air.

He retires.

Enter WOLF.

MILDRED - How now, Master Wolf?

WOLF - Where's Master Touchstone? I must speak with him presently; I have lost my breath for haste.

MILDRED - What's the matter, sir? Pray all be well.

WOLF - Master Deputy Golding is arrested upon an execution, and desires him presently to come to him forthwith.

MILDRED - Ay me! do you hear, Father?

TOUCHSTONE - [within] Tricks, tricks, confederacy, tricks! I have 'em in my nose — I scent 'em!

WOLF - Who's that? Master Touchstone?

MISTRESS TOUCHSTONE - Why, it is Master Wolf himself, husband.

MILDRED - Father!

TOUCHSTONE - [within] I am deaf still, I say. I will neither yield to the song of the siren nor the voice of the hyena, the tears of the crocodile nor the howling o' the Wolf: avoid my habitation, monsters!

WOLF - Why, you are not mad, sir? I pray you look forth and see the token I have brought you, sir.

TOUCHSTONE - [coming forward] Ha! what token is it?

WOLF - [aside to TOUCHSTONE] Do you know it, sir?

TOUCHSTONE - [aside] My son Golding's ring! Are you in earnest, Master Wolf?

WOLF - [aside] Ay, by my faith, sir. He is in prison, and requir'd me to use all speed and secrecy to you.

TOUCHSTONE - My cloak there (pray you be patient). — I am plagu'd for my austerity. — My cloak! — At whose suit, Master Wolf?

Exeunt.

WOLF - I'll tell you as we go, sir.

SCENE V – A YARD IN THE COUNTER

Enter FRIEND and the two PRISONERS.

FRIEND - Why, but is his offence such as he cannot hope of life?

1ST PRISONER - Troth, it should seem so; and 't is a great pity, for he is exceeding penitent.

FRIEND - They say he is charg'd but on suspicion of felony yet.

2ND PRISONER - Ay, but his master is a shrewd fellow; he'll prove great matter against him.

FRIEND - I'd as lief as anything I could see his "Farewell."

1ST PRISONER - Oh, 't is rarely written; why, Toby may get him to sing it to you; he's not curious to anybody.

2ND PRISONER - Oh, no! He would that all the world should take knowledge of his repentance, and thinks he merits in 't, the more shame he suffers.

1ST PRISONER - Pray thee, try what thou canst do.

2ND PRISONER - I warrant you he will not deny it, if he be not hoarse with the often repeating of it.

Exit.

1ST PRISONER - You never saw a more courteous creature than he is; and the knight too: the poorest prisoner of the house may command 'em. You shall hear a thing admirably penn'd.

FRIEND - Is the knight any scholar too?

1ST PRISONER - No, but he will speak very well, and discourse admirably of running horses and Whitefriars, and against bawds, and of cocks; and talk as loud as a hunter, but is none.

Enter WOLF and TOUCHSTONE.

WOLF - Please you stay here, sir; I'll call his Worship down to you.

Exit WOLF; TOUCHSTONE stands aside.

1ST PRISONER - See, he has brought him, and the knight too. Salute him.

Re-enter Second PRISONER with QUICKSILVER and PETRONEL; re-enter WOLF with GOLDING, and they stand aside.

1ST PRISONER - I pray, sir, this gentleman, upon our report, is very desirous to hear some piece of your "Repentance."

QUICKSILVER - Sir, with all my heart; and, as I told Master Toby, I shall be glad to have any man a witness of it; and, the more openly I profess it, I hope it will appear the heartier, and the more unfeigned.

TOUCHSTONE - [aside] Who is this? my man Francis and my son-in-law?

QUICKSILVER - Sir, it is all the testimony I shall leave behind me to the world and my master that I have so offended.

FRIEND - Good sir!

QUICKSILVER - I writ it when my spirits were oppress'd.

SIR PETRONEL - Ay, I'll be sworn for you, Francis.

QUICKSILVER - It is in imitation of Mannington's, he that was hang'd at Cambridge, that cut off the horse's head at a blow.

FRIEND - So, sir!

QUICKSILVER - To the tune of "I wail in woe, I plunge in pain."

SIR PETRONEL - An excellent ditty it is, and worthy of a new tune.
Quick.
In Cheapside, famous for gold and plate,
Quicksilver, I did dwell of late;
I had a master good and kind,
That would have wrought me to his mind.
He bade me still, "Work upon that";
But, alas! I wrought I knew not what.
He was a Touchstone, black, but true,
And told me still what would ensue;
Yet woe is me! I would not learn;
I saw, alas! but could not discern!

FRIEND - Excellent, excellent well!

GOLDING - [aside] O, let him alone. He is taken already.
Quick.
I cast my coat and cap away;
I went in silks and satins gay;
False metal of good manners I
Did daily coin unlawfully;
I scorn'd my master, being drunk;
I kept my gelding and my punk;
And with a knight, Sir Flash by name,
Who now is sorry for the same —

SIR PETRONEL - I thank you, Francis.
Quick.
I thought by sea to run away,
But Thames and tempest did me stay.

TOUCHSTONE - [aside] This cannot be feigned sure. Heaven pardon my severity! "The ragged colt
may prove a good horse."

GOLDING - [aside] How he listens! and is transported! He has forgot me.
Quick.
Still "Eastward Ho" was all my word;
But westward I had no regard,
Nor never thought what would come after,
As did, alas! his youngest daughter.
At last the black ox trod o' my foot,
And I saw then what 'long'd unto 't;
Now cry I, "Touchstone, touch me still,
And make me current by thy skill."

TOUCHSTONE - [aside] And I will do it, Francis.

WOLF - [aside to GOLDING] Stay him, Master Deputy; now is the time: we shall lose the song else.

FRIEND - I protest it is the best that ever I heard.

QUICKSILVER - How like you it, gentlemen?

ALL - Oh, admirable, sir!

QUICKSILVER - This stanza now following alludes to the story of Mannington, from whence I took my project for my invention.

FRIEND - Pray you go on, sir.
Quick.
O Mannington, thy stories show,
Thou cutt'st a horse-head off at a blow.
But I confess I have not the force
For to cut off the head of a horse;
Yet I desire this grace to win,
That I may cut off the horse-head of Sin,
And leave his body in the dust
Of sin's highway and bogs of lust,
Whereby I may take Virtue's purse,
And live with her for better, for worse.

FRIEND - Admirable, sir, and excellently conceited!

QUICKSILVER - Alas, sir!

TOUCHSTONE - [aside] Son Golding and Master Wolf, I thank you: the deceit is welcome, especially from thee, whose charitable soul in this hath shown a high point of wisdom and honesty. Listen, I am ravished with his repentance, and could stand here a whole prenticeship to hear him.

FRIEND - Forth, good sir.

QUICKSILVER - This is the last, and the "Farewell."
Farewell, Cheapside; farewell, sweet trade
Of goldsmiths all, that never shall fade;
Farewell, dear fellow prentices all,
And be you warned by my fall:
Shun usurers, bawds, and dice, and drabs;
Avoid them as you would French scabs.
Seek not to go beyond your tether,
But cut your thongs unto your leather;
So shall you thrive by little and little,
Scape Tyburn, Counters, and the Spital.

TOUCHSTONE - [coming forward] And scape them shalt thou, my penitent and dear Francis!

QUICKSILVER - Master!

SIR PETRONEL - Father!

TOUCHSTONE - I can no longer forbear to do your humility right. Arise, and let me honor your repentance with the hearty and joyful embraces of a father and friend's love. Quicksilver, thou hast ate into my breast, Quicksilver, with the drops of thy sorrow, and kill'd the desperate opinion I had of thy reclaim.

QUICKSILVER - Oh, sir, I am not worthy to see your worshipful face!

SIR PETRONEL - Forgive me, Father.

TOUCHSTONE - Speak no more; all former passages are forgotten; and here my word shall release you. — Thank this worthy brother, and kind friend, Francis. — Master Wolf, I am their bail.

A shout in the prison, and SECURITY appears at the grating.

SECURITY - Master Touchstone! Master Touchstone!

TOUCHSTONE - Who's that?

WOLF - Security, sir.

SECURITY - Pray you, sir, if you'll be won with a song, hear my lamentable tune too:

SONG
O Master Touchstone,
My heart is full of woe;
Alas, I am a cuckold!
And why should it be so?
Because I was a usurer
And bawd, as all you know;
For which, again I tell you,
My heart is full of woe.

TOUCHSTONE - Bring him forth, Master Wolf, and release his bands. This day shall be sacred to mercy, and the mirth of this encounter in the Counter. — See, we are encount'red with more suitors.

Enter MISTRESS TOUCHSTONE, GERTRUDE, MILDRED, SINDEFY, and WINIFRED; and WOLF with SECURITY.

Save your breath, save your breath! All things have succeeded to your wishes; and we are heartily satisifed in their events.

GERTRUDE - Ah, runaway, runaway! have I caught you? And how has my poor knight done all this while?

SIR PETRONEL - Dear Lady-wife, forgive me!

GERTRUDE - As heartily as I would be forgiven, knight. Dear Father, give me your blessing, and forgive me too; I ha' been proud and lascivious, Father; and a fool, Father; and, being rais'd to the state of a wanton coy thing, call'd a lady, Father, have scorn'd you, Father, and my sister, and my sister's velvet cap, too, and would make a mouth at the city as I rid through it, and stop mine ears at

Bow-bell. I have said your beard was a base one, Father; and that you looked like Twierpipe, the taborer; and that my mother was but my midwife.

MISTRESS TOUCHSTONE - Now, God forgi' you, child madam!

TOUCHSTONE - No more repetitions. What is else wanting to make our harmony full?

GOLDING - Only this, sir, that my fellow Francis make amends to Mistress Sindefy with marriage.

QUICKSILVER - With all my heart.

GOLDING - And Security give her a dower, which shall be all the restitution he shall make of that huge mass he hath so unlawfully gotten.

TOUCHSTONE - Excellently devis'd! a good motion! What says Master Security?

SECURITY - I say anything, sir, what you'll ha' me say. Would I were no cuckold!

WINIFRED - Cuckold, husband? Why, I think this wearing of yellow has infected you.

TOUCHSTONE - Why, Master Security, that should rather be a comfort to you than a corrosive. If you be a cuckold, it's an argument you have a beautiful woman to your wife; then you shall be much made of; you shall have store of friends, never want money; you shall be eas'd of much o' your wedlock pain; others will take it for you. Besides, you being a usurer, and likely to go to hell, the devils will never torment you: they'll take you for one o' their own race. Again, if you be a cuckold, and know it not, you are an innocent; if you know it and endure it, a true martyr.

SECURITY - I am resolv'd, sir. Come hither, Winny.

TOUCHSTONE - Well, then, all are pleas'd; or shall be anon. Master Wolf, you look hungry, methinks. Have you no apparel to lend Francis, to shift him?

QUICKSILVER - No, sir, nor I desire none; but here make it my suit that I may go home, through the streets in these, as a spectacle, or rather an example, to the children of Cheapside.

TOUCHSTONE - Thou hast thy wish. Now, London, look about,
And in this moral see thy glass run out:
Behold the careful father, thrifty son,
The solemn deeds, which each of us have done;
The usurer punish'd, and from fall so steep
The prodigal child reclaim'd, and the lost sheep.

EPILOGUS

QUICKSILVER - Stay, sir, I perceive the multitude are gather'd together to view our coming out at the Counter. See, if the streets and the fronts of the houses be not stuck with people, and the windows fill'd with ladies, as on the solemn day of the pageant! —
Oh, may you find in this our pageant here,
The same contentment which you came to seek;

And, as that show but draws you once a year,
May this attract you hither once a week.

Exeunt.

Ben Jonson – A Short Biography

Ben Jonson was born on either (by most accounts) June 9th or June 11th, 1572 in Westminster, London.

Jonson later recounted that his father (who died before he was born) had been a prosperous Protestant landowner until the reign of "Bloody Mary" and had suffered imprisonment and the forfeiture of his wealth during that monarch's attempt to restore England to Catholicism. On Elizabeth's accession he was freed and was able to travel to London to become a clergyman. His widowed mother remarried two years after his death.

Jonson's education began in a small church school attached to St Martin-in-the-Fields parish, and at the age of about seven he secured a place at Westminster School. It is attributed that a family friend paid for his studies at Westminster, where the antiquarian, historian, topographer, and officer of arms, William Camden was a master. Pupil and master became great friends, and Camden's broad range of interests and teachings had a great influence on Jonson throughout Camden's life.

On leaving Westminster School, Cambridge beckoned but instead Jonson was apprenticed to his bricklayer stepfather. After this apprenticeship Jonson travelled to the Netherlands and signed up as a volunteer with the English regiments of Francis Vere (1560–1609), in Flanders.

The later Hawthornden Manuscripts (1619), that recorded the conversations between Ben Jonson and the poet William Drummond of Hawthornden (1585–1649), report that, when in Flanders, Jonson engaged, fought, and killed an enemy soldier in single combat, and took for trophies the weapons of the vanquished soldier. After his military activity on the Continent, Jonson returned to England and worked as an actor and a playwright.

As an actor, Jonson was the protagonist "Hieronimo" (Geronimo) in the play The Spanish Tragedy, by Thomas Kyd (1558–94), the first revenge tragedy in English literature.

Naturally certainty in the details of these times is difficult. He appears to have married a "a shrew, yet honest" woman, sometimes attributed as Ann(e) Lewis at the church of St Magnus-the-Matyr near London Bridge in 1594 though other accounts give November 1593 as the date of the death of their 6 month old daughter Mary (immortalised in the heart breaking poem "On My First Daughter"), suggesting the marriage was somewhat earlier.

By the summer of 1597, Jonson had a fixed engagement in the Admiral's Men, performing under Philip Henslowe, then the leading producer for the English public theatre, at The Rose. Jonson appears not to have been much of an actor but showed potential as a writer.

His early forays as playwright were tragedies but none are recorded as surviving. An undated comedy 'The Case is Altered' is thought to be the earliest.

Jonson was not shy of causing controversy and many of his views courted it easily. In 1597 a play which he co-wrote with Thomas Nashe, The Isle of Dogs, was suppressed after causing great offence. Warrants for the arrest of Jonson and Nashe were issued by Queen Elizabeth I's interrogator, Richard Topcliffe.

Jonson was jailed in Marshalsea Prison and charged with "Leude and mutynous behavior", while Nashe managed to escape to Great Yarmouth. Two of the actors, Gabriel Spenser and Robert Shaw, were also imprisoned.

In 1598 Jonson produced his first great success, Every Man in His Humour, capitalising on the fashion for comedic plays which George Chapman had begun with An Humorous Day's Mirth. A certain William Shakespeare was among the first actors to be cast.

A year later, Jonson was again briefly imprisoned, this time in Newgate Prison, for killing Gabriel Spenser in a duel on 22 September 1598 in Hogsden Fields. Tried on a charge of manslaughter, Jonson would plead guilty but be released by benefit of clergy, a legal ploy through which he gained leniency by reciting a brief bible verse (the neck-verse), forfeiting his 'goods and chattels' and being branded on his left thumb.

But during his time Jonson's faith was to play a further complicating part in this difficult situation. Brought up in the Protestant faith, he had maintained an interest in Catholic doctrine throughout his adult life and, at this perilous time when a religious war with Spain was expected and persecution of Catholics was intensifying, he converted to the Catholic faith in October 1598 (while he was still on remand in Newgate). It was a unique combination of events and obviously a difficult choice.

It has been suggested that the conversion was instigated by Father Thomas Wright, a former Jesuit priest who had resigned from the order over his acceptance of Queen Elizabeth's right to rule in England. Wright, although placed under house arrest on the orders of Lord Burghley, was permitted to minister to the inmates of London prisons. It may have been that Jonson, fearing that his trial would go against him, was seeking the unequivocal absolution that Catholicism could offer if he were sentenced to death. Or, almost equally, he could have been looking to personal advantage from accepting conversion since Father Wright's protector, the Earl of Essex, was among those who might hope to rise to influence after the succession of a new monarch. The argument was that the royal succession, from the childless Elizabeth, had not been settled and Essex's Catholic allies were hopeful that a sympathetic ruler might attain the throne.

Either way, Jonson was now released and his artistic life was the main channel of his activity. This continued to flower and in 1599, Every Man Out of His Humour, was performed on stage. When it was published it proved popular and went through several editions.

Jonson's other work for the theatre in the last years of Elizabeth I's reign was marked by fighting and controversy. Cynthia's Revels was produced by the Children of the Chapel Royal at Blackfriars Theatre in 1600. It satirised both John Marston, who Jonson believed had accused him of lustfulness, possibly in Histrio Mastix, and Thomas Dekker. Jonson attacked the two poets again in 1601's Poetaster. Dekker responded with Satiromastix, subtitled "the untrussing of the humorous poet".

This "War of the Theatres" seems to have ended with reconciliation on all sides. Jonson collaborated with Dekker on a pageant welcoming James I to England in 1603 although Drummond reports that Jonson called Dekker a rogue. Marston dedicated The Malcontent to Jonson.

Tragically, that same 1603, Benjamin Jonson, his eldest son, died of Bubonic plague at the age of seven; to lament and honour the dead boy, Jonson wrote the elegiac On My First Sonne.

With the new King, James I, on the throne Jonson quickly saw the need for and demand for masques and entertainments which was also promoted by both the king and his consort Anne of Denmark. In addition to his popularity on the public stage and in the royal hall, he enjoyed the patronage of aristocrats such as Elizabeth Sidney (daughter of Sir Philip Sidney) and Lady Mary Wroth. This connection with the Sidney family provided the impetus for one of Jonson's most famous lyrics, the country house poem To Penshurst.

In February 1603 John Manningham reported that Jonson was living at Robert Townsend's, son of Sir Roger Townshend, and "scorns the world." This provides a plausible and reasonable explanation as to why his troubles with English authorities continued. That same year he was questioned by the Privy Council about Sejanus, a politically themed play about corruption in the Roman Empire. Conviction, and certainly not expedience alone, sustained Jonson's faith during the troublesome twelve years he remained a Catholic. His stance received attention beyond the state intolerance to which most faithful followers were exposed. That first draft of Sejanus was banned for "popery", and did not re-appear until the offending passages were cut.

At the same time, Jonson pursued a more prestigious career, writing masques for James's court. The Satyr (1603) and The Masque of Blackness (1605) are two of about two dozen masques which Jonson wrote for James or for Queen Anne; The Masque of Blackness was praised by Algernon Charles Swinburne as the consummate example of this now-extinct genre, which mingled speech, dancing, and spectacle.

In 1605 Jonson collaborated with Chapman on Eastward Ho, a play whose anti-Scottish sentiment landed both authors in jail for a short time to bring home to them the authorities displeasure with their work. Shortly after he was, unfortunately, present at a supper party attended by most of the Gunpowder Plot conspirators.

With the plot's discovery he seems to have avoided further imprisonment by volunteering what he knew to the investigator Robert Cecil and the Privy Council. Father Thomas Wright, who heard Fawkes's confession, was known to Jonson from prison in 1598 and Cecil may have directed him to bring the priest before the council, as a witness.

Now, in January 1606, Jonson (with his wife Anne) appeared before the Consistory Court to answer a charge of recusancy, with Jonson additionally accused of allowing his fame as a Catholic to "seduce" citizens to the cause. This was a serious matter, especially as the Gunpowder Plot was only a few moths before, but he explained that his failure to take communion was only because he had not found sound theological endorsement for the practice. By paying a fine of thirteen shillings he escaped the more serious penalties available to the authorities. His habit was to slip outside during the sacrament, a common routine at the time—indeed it was one followed by Queen Anne, herself —to show political loyalty whilst not offending the conscience. Leading church figures, including John Overall, Dean of St Paul's, were directed to win Jonson back to orthodoxy, but these overtures met no success.

Jonson's poetry, as is his drama, is informed by his classical learning. Some of his better-known poems are close translations of Greek or Roman models; all display a careful attention to form and style that often came naturally to those trained in classics. Jonson largely avoided debate about rhyme and meter that had consumed other Elizabethan classicists. Accepting both rhyme and stress, Jonson used them to mimic the classical qualities of simplicity, restraint, and precision.

In May 1610 King Henri IV of France, a Catholic monarch respected in England for tolerance towards Protestants, was assassinated, purportedly in the name of the Pope, and this seems to have been the immediate cause of Jonson's decision to rejoin the Church of England. He did this in flamboyant style, pointedly drinking a full chalice of communion wine at the eucharist to demonstrate his renunciation of the Catholic rite, in which the priest alone drinks the wine. Despite this very public display his interest in Catholic belief and practice remained with him until his death.

On ensuing projects he collaborated, not always peacefully, with the designer Inigo Jones. For example, Jones designed the scenery for Jonson's masque Oberon, the Faery Prince performed at Whitehall on 1 January 1611 in which Prince Henry, eldest son of James I, appeared in the title role.

Perhaps partly as a result of this new career, Jonson gave up writing plays for the public theatres for a decade. He later told Drummond that he had made less than two hundred pounds on all his plays together.

The period between 1605 and 1620 may mow be viewed as Jonson's golden period. By 1616 he had produced all the plays on which his present reputation as a dramatist is based, including the tragedy Catiline (acted and printed 1611), which achieved limited success, and the comedies Volpone, (acted 1605, printed in 1607), Epicoene, or the Silent Woman (1609), The Alchemist (1610), Bartholomew Fair (1614) and The Devil is an Ass (1616). The Alchemist and Volpone were immediately successful. Epicoene, Bartholomew Fair and (to a lesser extent) The Devil is an Ass have, in modern times, achieved a greater degree of recognition. During this period his life was more settled and without so much of the excess and controversy of former years but, despite this success, his financial security was still not assured.

In 1616 Jonson received a yearly pension of 100 marks (about £60), and was also appointed as Poet Laureate (though this Post was long standing it was, at the time, an unofficial position). This sign of royal favour may have encouraged him to publish the first volume of the folio collected edition of his works that year. Other volumes were to follow much later.

Included in the 1615 folio are "Epigrams", a genre popular among late-Elizabethan and Jacobean audiences, although Jonson was perhaps the only poet of his time to work in its full classical range. The epigrams explore various attitudes, most from the satiric stock of the day: complaints against women, courtiers, and spies abound. The condemnatory poems are short and anonymous; Jonson's epigrams of praise, including a famous poem to Camden and lines to Lucy Harington, are longer and are mostly addressed to specific individuals. Although it is included among the epigrams, "On My First Sonne" is neither satirical nor very short; the poem, intensely personal and deeply felt, typifies a genre that would evolve itself to be called "lyric poetry." Jonson's poems of "The Forest" also appeared in the first folio. Most of the fifteen poems are addressed to Jonson's aristocratic supporters, but the most famous are his country-house poem "To Penshurst" and the poem "To Celia" ("Come, my Celia, let us prove") that appears also in Volpone.

Jonson set out in 1618 for his ancestral Scotland on foot. He spent over a year there, and the best-remembered hospitality which he enjoyed was that of the Scottish poet, William Drummond of Hawthornden, in April 1619, sited on the River Esk. Drummond undertook to record as much of Jonson's conversation as he could in his diary, and thus recorded aspects of Jonson's personality that might otherwise have been lost. Jonson delivers his opinions, in Drummond's terse reporting, in an expansive and even magisterial mood. Drummond noted he was "a great lover and praiser of himself, a contemner and scorner of others".

In Edinburgh he was made an honorary citizen of Edinburgh.

From there he travelled west and lodged with the Duke of Lennox where he wrote a play based on Loch Lomond.

On returning to England, he was awarded an honorary Master of Arts degree from Oxford University.

Jonson's creativity began to decline in the 1620s. He was still well-known and many looked up to him as both mentor and for guidance. These were called the "Sons of Ben" or the "Tribe of Ben", in their number were poets such as Robert Herrick, Richard Lovelace, and Sir John Suckling who took their bearing in verse from Jonson. Though his strength and reputation were waning he did resume writing regular plays. Although these failed to emulate his former gems they do have interesting angles, especially of Charles I. The Staple of News also offers a remarkable look at the earliest stage of English journalism.

In 1623, historian Edmund Bolton named him the best and most polished English poet. That this judgment was widely shared is indicated by the admitted influence he had on younger poets. The grounds for describing Jonson as the "father" of cavalier poets are clear: as noted previously, many of the cavalier poets described themselves as his "sons" or his "tribe". For some of them, the connection was as much social as poetic; Herrick described meetings at "the Sun, the Dog, the Triple Tunne". All of them, including those like Herrick whose accomplishments in verse are generally regarded as superior to Jonson's, took inspiration from Jonson's revival of classical forms and themes, his subtle melodies, and his disciplined use of wit. In these respects Jonson may be regarded as among the most important figures in the history of English neoclassicism.

The principal factor in Jonson's partial eclipse was the death of James and the accession of King Charles I in 1625. Jonson felt neglected by the new court. A decisive quarrel with Jones harmed his career as a writer of court masques, although he continued to entertain the court on an irregular basis. For his part, Charles displayed a certain affection for the great poet of his father's day: he therefore increased Jonson's annual pension to £100 and included a tierce of wine.

Family tragedy struck again in 1635 when a second son, also named Benjamin Jonson, died. In that period, Ann Lewis and Ben Jonson lived separate lives for several years; their martial arrangement cast Ann Lewis as the housewife Jonson, and Ben Jonson as the artist who enjoyed the residential hospitality of his patrons, Sir Robert Townshend and Lord Aubigny, Esme Stuart, 3rd Duke of Lennox.

Ben Jonson died on August 6[th,] 1637. At his death he seems to have been working on another play, The Sad Shepherd. Though only two acts are extant, this represents a remarkable new direction for Jonson: a move into pastoral drama.

His funeral was held on August 9th. He is buried in the north aisle of the nave in Westminster Abbey, with the inscription "O Rare Ben Johnson" set in the slab over his grave.

The fact that Jonson was buried in an upright position was either an indication of his reduced circumstances at the time of his death, or, alternatively it has been written that he asked for a grave exactly 18 inches square from the monarch and received an upright grave to fit in the requested space.

There is a suggestion that the inscription could be read "Orare Ben Jonson" (pray for Ben Jonson), which would fit on many religious levels on the soul but the carving shows a distinct space between "O" and "rare".

In 1723 a monument to Jonson was erected by the Earl of Oxford and is in the eastern aisle of Westminster Abbey's Poets' Corner. It includes a portrait medallion and the same inscription as on the gravestone. It seems Jonson was to have had a monument erected by subscription soon after his death but with the advent of the English Civil War this did not happen.

In summing up Ben Jonson was a classically educated, well-read, and cultured man of the English Renaissance with a large appetite for controversy (personal and political, artistic and intellectual) whose cultural influence was of unparalleled breadth upon the playwrights and the poets of the Jacobean era (1603–1625) and of the Caroline era (1625–1642).

During the 17th century Jonson was a towering literary figure, and he has been described as 'One of the most vigorous minds that ever added to the strength of English literature'. Before the English Civil War, the "Tribe of Ben" touted his importance, and during the Restoration Jonson's satirical comedies and his theory and practice of "humour characters" was extremely influential, providing the model for many Restoration comedies.

In the 18th century Jonson's status began to decline and by the Romantic era, Jonson suffered the fate of being unfairly compared and contrasted to Shakespeare. It is only now, hundred of years later that his true worth can be assessed and he can be placed in the very front rank of English literary figures.

Ben Jonson – A Concise Bibliography

Plays

A Tale of a Tub, comedy (c. 1596 revised, performed 1633)
The Isle of Dogs, comedy (1597, with Thomas Nashe)
The Case is Altered, comedy (c. 1597–98), with Henry Porter and Anthony Munday
Every Man in His Humour, comedy (performed 1598)
Every Man out of His Humour, comedy (performed 1599)
Cynthia's Revels (performed 1600)
The Poetaster, comedy (performed 1601)
Sejanus His Fall, tragedy (performed 1603)
Eastward Ho, comedy (performed 1605), a collaboration with John Marston and George Chapman
Volpone, comedy (c. 1605–06)
Epicoene, or the Silent Woman, comedy (performed)
The Alchemist, comedy (performed 1610)
Catiline His Conspiracy, tragedy (performed 1611)
Bartholomew Fair, comedy (performed 31 October 1614)
The Devil is an Ass, comedy (performed 1616)
The Staple of News, comedy (performed February 1626)
The New Inn, or The Light Heart, comedy (licensed 19 January 1629)
The Magnetic Lady, or Humors Reconciled, comedy (licensed 12 October 1632)
The Sad Shepherd, pastoral (c. 1637), unfinished
Mortimer His Fall, history (printed 1641), a fragment

Masques

The Coronation Triumph, or The King's Entertainment (performed 15 March 1604) with Thomas Dekker

A Private Entertainment of the King and Queen on May-Day (The Penates) (1 May 1604)
The Entertainment of the Queen and Prince Henry at Althorp (The Satyr) (25 June 1603)
The Masque of Blackness (6 January 1605)
Hymenaei (5 January 1606)
The Entertainment of the Kings of Great Britain and Denmark (The Hours) (24 July 1606)
The Masque of Beauty (10 January 1608)
The Masque of Queens (2 February 1609)
The Hue and Cry After Cupid, or The Masque at Lord Haddington's Marriage (9 February 1608)
The Entertainment at Britain's Burse (11 April 1609)
The Speeches at Prince Henry's Barriers, or The Lady of the Lake (6 January 1610)
Oberon, the Faery Prince (1 January 1611)
Love Freed from Ignorance and Folly (3 February 1611)
Love Restored (6 January 1612)
A Challenge at Tilt, at a Marriage (27 December 1613/1 January 1614)
The Irish Masque at Court (29 December 1613)
Mercury Vindicated from the Alchemists (6 January 1615)
The Golden Age Restored (1 January 1616)
Christmas, His Masque (Christmas 1616)
The Vision of Delight (6 January 1617)
Lovers Made Men, or The Masque of Lethe, or The Masque at Lord Hay's (22 February 1617)
Pleasure Reconciled to Virtue (6 January 1618) The masque was a failure; Jonson revised it by placing the anti-masque first, turning it into:-
For the Honour of Wales (17 February 1618)
News from the New World Discovered in the Moon (7 January 1620)
The Entertainment at Blackfriars, or The Newcastle Entertainment (May 1620)
Pan's Anniversary, or The Shepherd's Holy-Day (19 June 1620)
The Gypsies Metamorphosed (3 and 5 August 1621)
The Masque of Augurs (6 January 1622)
Time Vindicated to Himself and to His Honours (19 January 1623)
Neptune's Triumph for the Return of Albion (26 January 1624)
The Masque of Owls at Kenilworth (19 August 1624)
The Fortunate Isles and Their Union (9 January 1625)
Love's Triumph Through Callipolis (9 January 1631)
Chloridia: Rites to Chloris and Her Nymphs (22 February 1631)
The King's Entertainment at Welbeck in Nottinghamshire (21 May 1633)
Love's Welcome at Bolsover (30 July 1634)

Other Works
Epigrams (1612)
The Forest (1616), including To Penshurst
On My First Sonne (1616), elegy
A Discourse of Love (1618)
Barclay's Argenis, translated by Jonson (1623)
The Execration against Vulcan (1640)
Horace's Art of Poetry, translated by Jonson (1640)
Underwood (1640)
English Grammar (1640)
Timber, or Discoveries made upon men and matter, as they have flowed out of his daily readings, or had their reflux to his peculiar notion of the times, a commonplace book
To Celia (Drink to Me Only With Thine Eyes), poem

The greatest of English dramatists except Shakespeare, the first literary dictator and poet-laureate, a writer of verse, prose, satire, and criticism who most potently of all the men of his time affected the subsequent course of English letters: such was Ben Jonson, and as such his strong personality assumes an interest to us almost unparalleled, at least in his age.

Ben Jonson came of the stock that was centuries after to give to the world Thomas Carlyle; for Jonson's grandfather was of Annandale, over the Solway, whence he migrated to England. Jonson's father lost his estate under Queen Mary, "having been cast into prison and forfeited." He entered the church, but died a month before his illustrious son was born, leaving his widow and child in poverty. Jonson's birthplace was Westminster, and the time of his birth early in 1573. He was thus nearly ten years Shakespeare's junior, and less well off, if a trifle better born. But Jonson did not profit even by this slight advantage. His mother married beneath her, a wright or bricklayer, and Jonson was for a time apprenticed to the trade. As a youth he attracted the attention of the famous antiquary, William Camden, then usher at Westminster School, and there the poet laid the solid foundations of his classical learning. Jonson always held Camden in veneration, acknowledging that to him he owed,

"All that I am in arts, all that I know;"

and dedicating his first dramatic success, "Every Man in His Humour," to him. It is doubtful whether Jonson ever went to either university, though Fuller says that he was "statutably admitted into St. John's College, Cambridge." He tells us that he took no degree, but was later "Master of Arts in both the universities, by their favour, not his study." When a mere youth Jonson enlisted as a soldier, trailing his pike in Flanders in the protracted wars of William the Silent against the Spanish. Jonson was a large and raw-boned lad; he became by his own account in time exceedingly bulky. In chat with his friend William Drummond of Hawthornden, Jonson told how "in his service in the Low Countries he had, in the face of both the camps, killed an enemy, and taken opima spolia from him;" and how "since his coming to England, being appealed to the fields, he had killed his adversary which had hurt him in the arm and whose sword was ten inches longer than his." Jonson's reach may have made up for the lack of his sword; certainly his prowess lost nothing in the telling. Obviously Jonson was brave, combative, and not averse to talking of himself and his doings.

In 1592, Jonson returned from abroad penniless. Soon after he married, almost as early and quite as imprudently as Shakespeare. He told Drummond curtly that "his wife was a shrew, yet honest"; for some years he lived apart from her in the household of Lord Albany. Yet two touching epitaphs among Jonson's "Epigrams," "On my first daughter," and "On my first son," attest the warmth of the poet's family affections. The daughter died in infancy, the son of the plague; another son grew up to manhood little credit to his father whom he survived. We know nothing beyond this of Jonson's domestic life.

How soon Jonson drifted into what we now call grandly "the theatrical profession" we do not know. In 1593, Marlowe made his tragic exit from life, and Greene, Shakespeare's other rival on the popular stage, had preceded Marlowe in an equally miserable death the year before. Shakespeare already had the running to himself. Jonson appears first in the employment of Philip Henslowe, the exploiter of several troupes of players, manager, and father-in-law of the famous actor, Edward Alleyn. From entries in "Henslowe's Diary," a species of theatrical account book which has been handed down to us, we know that Jonson was connected with the Admiral's men; for he borrowed 4 pounds of Henslowe, July 28, 1597, paying back 3s. 9d. on the same day on account of his "share" (in what is not altogether clear); while later, on December 3, of the same year, Henslowe advanced 20s. to him "upon a book which he showed the plot unto the company which he promised to deliver unto the company at Christmas next." In the next August Jonson was in collaboration with Chettle and Porter in a play called "Hot Anger Soon Cold." All this points to an association with Henslowe of some duration, as no mere tyro would be thus paid in advance upon mere promise. From allusions in Dekker's play, "Satiromastix," it appears that Jonson, like Shakespeare, began life as an actor, and that he "ambled in a leather pitch by a play-wagon" taking at one time the part of Hieronimo in Kyd's famous play, "The Spanish Tragedy." By the beginning of 1598, Jonson, though still in needy circumstances, had begun to receive recognition. Francis Meres -- well known for his "Comparative Discourse of our English Poets with the Greek, Latin, and Italian Poets," printed in 1598, and for his mention therein of a dozen plays of Shakespeare by title -- accords to Ben Jonson a place as one of "our best in tragedy," a matter of some surprise, as no known tragedy of Jonson from so early a date has come down to us. That Jonson was at work on tragedy, however, is proved by the entries in Henslowe of at least three tragedies, now lost, in which he had a hand. These are "Page of Plymouth," "King Robert II. of Scotland," and "Richard Crookback." But all of these came later, on his return to Henslowe, and range from August 1599 to June 1602.

Returning to the autumn of 1598, an event now happened to sever for a time Jonson's relations with Henslowe. In a letter to Alleyn, dated September 26 of that year, Henslowe writes: "I have lost one of my company that hurteth me greatly; that is Gabriel [Spencer], for he is slain in Hogsden fields by the hands of Benjamin Jonson, bricklayer." The last word is perhaps Henslowe's thrust at Jonson in his displeasure rather than a designation of his actual continuance at his trade up to this time. It is fair to Jonson to remark however, that his adversary appears to have been a notorious fire-eater who had shortly before killed one Feeke in a similar squabble. Duelling was a frequent occurrence of the time among gentlemen and the nobility; it was an impudent breach of the peace on the part of a player. This duel is the one which Jonson described years after to Drummond, and for it Jonson was duly arraigned at Old Bailey, tried, and convicted. He was sent to prison and such goods and chattels as he had "were forfeited." It is a thought to give one pause that, but for the ancient law permitting convicted felons to plead, as it was called, the benefit of clergy, Jonson might have been hanged for this deed. The circumstance that the poet could read and write saved him; and he received only a brand of the letter "T," for Tyburn, on his left thumb. While in jail Jonson became a Roman Catholic; but he returned to the faith of the Church of England a dozen years later.

On his release, in disgrace with Henslowe and his former associates, Jonson offered his services as a playwright to Henslowe's rivals, the Lord Chamberlain's company, in which Shakespeare was a prominent shareholder. A tradition of long standing, though not susceptible of proof in a court of law, narrates that Jonson had submitted the manuscript of "Every Man in His Humour" to the Chamberlain's men and had received from the company a refusal; that Shakespeare called him back, read the play himself, and at once accepted it. Whether this story is true or not, certain it is that "Every Man in His Humour" was accepted by Shakespeare's company and acted for the first time in 1598, with Shakespeare taking a part. The evidence of this is contained in the list of actors prefixed to the comedy in the folio of Jonson's works, 1616. But it is a mistake to infer, because Shakespeare's name stands first in the list of actors and the elder Kno'well first in the dramatis personae, that Shakespeare took that particular part. The order of a list of Elizabethan players was generally that of their importance or priority as shareholders in the company and seldom if ever corresponded to the list of characters.

"Every Man in His Humour" was an immediate success, and with it Jonson's reputation as one of the leading dramatists of his time was established once and for all. This could have been by no means Jonson's earliest comedy, and we have just learned that he was already reputed one of "our best in tragedy." Indeed, one of Jonson's extant comedies, "The Case is Altered," but one never claimed by him or published as his, must certainly have preceded "Every Man in His Humour" on the stage. The former play may be described as a comedy modelled on the Latin plays of Plautus. (It combines, in fact, situations derived from the "Captivi" and the "Aulularia" of that dramatist). But the pretty story of the beggar-maiden, Rachel, and her suitors, Jonson found, not among the classics, but in the ideals of romantic love which Shakespeare had already popularised on the stage. Jonson never again produced so fresh and lovable a feminine personage as Rachel, although in other respects "The Case is Altered" is not a conspicuous play, and, save for the satirising of Antony Munday in the person of Antonio Balladino and Gabriel Harvey as well, is perhaps the least characteristic of the comedies of Jonson.

"Every Man in His Humour," probably first acted late in the summer of 1598 and at the Curtain, is commonly regarded as an epoch-making play; and this view is not unjustified. As to plot, it tells little more than how an intercepted letter enabled a father to follow his supposedly studious son to London, and there observe his life with the gallants of the time. The real quality of this comedy is in its personages and in the theory upon which they are conceived. Ben Jonson had theories about poetry and the drama, and he was neither chary in talking of them nor in experimenting with them in his plays. This makes Jonson, like Dryden in his time, and Wordsworth much later, an author to reckon with; particularly when we remember that many of Jonson's notions came for a time definitely to prevail and to modify the whole trend of English poetry. First of all Jonson was a classicist, that is, he believed in restraint and precedent in art in opposition to the prevalent ungoverned and irresponsible Renaissance spirit. Jonson believed that there was a professional way of doing things which might be reached by a study of the best examples, and he found these examples for the most part among the ancients. To confine our attention to the drama, Jonson objected to the amateurishness and haphazard nature of many contemporary plays, and set himself to do something different; and the first and most striking thing that he evolved was his conception and practice of the comedy of humours.

As Jonson has been much misrepresented in this matter, let us quote his own words as to "humour." A humour, according to Jonson, was a bias of disposition, a warp, so to speak, in character by which

"Some one peculiar quality
Doth so possess a man, that it doth draw
All his affects, his spirits, and his powers,
In their confluctions, all to run one way."

But continuing, Jonson is careful to add:

"But that a rook by wearing a pied feather,
The cable hat-band, or the three-piled ruff,
A yard of shoe-tie, or the Switzers knot
On his French garters, should affect a humour!
O, it is more than most ridiculous."

Jonson's comedy of humours, in a word, conceived of stage personages on the basis of a ruling trait or passion (a notable simplification of actual life be it observed in passing); and, placing these typified traits in juxtaposition in their conflict and contrast, struck the spark of comedy. Downright, as his name indicates, is "a plain squire"; Bobadill's humour is that of the braggart who is incidentally, and with delightfully comic effect, a coward; Brainworm's humour is the finding out of things to the end of fooling everybody: of course he is fooled in the end himself. But it was not Jonson's theories alone that made the success of "Every Man in His Humour." The play is admirably written and each character is vividly conceived, and with a firm touch based on observation of the men of the London of the day. Jonson was neither in this, his first great comedy (nor in any other play that he wrote), a supine classicist, urging that English drama return to a slavish adherence to classical conditions. He says as to the laws of the old comedy (meaning by "laws," such matters as the unities of time and place and the use of chorus): "I see not then, but we should enjoy the same licence, or free power to illustrate and heighten our invention as they [the ancients] did; and not be tied to those strict and regular forms which the niceness of a few, who are nothing but form, would thrust upon us." "Every Man in His Humour" is written in prose, a novel practice which Jonson had of his predecessor in comedy, John Lyly. Even the word "humour" seems to have been employed in the Jonsonian sense by Chapman before Jonson's use of it. Indeed, the comedy of humours itself is only a heightened variety of the comedy of manners which represents life, viewed at a satirical angle, and is the oldest and most persistent species of comedy in the language. None the less, Jonson's comedy merited its immediate success and marked out a definite course in which comedy long continued to run. To mention only Shakespeare's Falstaff and his rout, Bardolph, Pistol, Dame Quickly, and the rest, whether in "Henry IV." or in "The Merry Wives of Windsor," all are conceived in the spirit of humours. So are the captains, Welsh, Scotch, and Irish of "Henry V.," and Malvolio especially later; though Shakespeare never employed the method of humours for an important personage. It was not Jonson's fault that many of his successors did precisely the thing that he had reprobated, that is, degrade the humour: into an oddity of speech, an eccentricity of manner, of dress, or cut of beard. There was an anonymous play called "Every Woman in Her Humour." Chapman wrote "A Humourous Day's Mirth," Day, "Humour Out of Breath," Fletcher later, "The Humourous Lieutenant," and Jonson, besides "Every Man Out of His Humour," returned to the title in closing the cycle of his comedies in "The Magnetic Lady or Humours Reconciled."

With the performance of "Every Man Out of His Humour" in 1599, by Shakespeare's company once more at the Globe, we turn a new page in Jonson's career. Despite his many real virtues, if there is one feature more than any other that distinguishes Jonson, it is his arrogance; and to this may be added his self-righteousness, especially under criticism or satire. "Every Man Out of His Humour" is the first of three "comical satires" which Jonson contributed to what Dekker called the poetomachia or war of the theatres as recent critics have named it. This play as a fabric of plot is a very slight affair; but as a satirical picture of the manners of the time, proceeding by means of vivid caricature, couched in witty and brilliant dialogue and sustained by that righteous indignation which must lie at the heart of all true satire -- as a realisation, in short, of the classical ideal of comedy -- there had been nothing like Jonson's comedy since the days of Aristophanes. "Every Man in His Humour," like the two plays that follow it, contains two kinds of attack, the critical or generally satiric, levelled at abuses and corruptions in the abstract; and the personal, in which specific application is made of all this in the lampooning of poets and others, Jonson's contemporaries. The method of personal attack by actual caricature of a person on the stage is almost as old as the drama. Aristophanes so lampooned Euripides in "The Acharnians" and Socrates in "The Clouds," to mention no other examples; and in English drama this kind of thing is alluded to again and again. What Jonson really did, was to raise the dramatic lampoon to an art, and make out of a casual burlesque and bit of mimicry a dramatic satire of literary pretensions and permanency. With the arrogant attitude mentioned above and his uncommon eloquence in scorn, vituperation, and invective, it is no wonder that Jonson soon involved himself in literary and even personal quarrels with his fellow-authors. The circumstances of the origin of this 'poetomachia' are far from clear, and those who have written on the topic, except of late, have not helped to make them clearer. The origin of the "war" has been referred to satirical references, apparently to Jonson, contained in "The Scourge of Villainy," a satire in regular form after the manner of the ancients by John Marston, a fellow playwright, subsequent friend and collaborator of Jonson's. On the other hand, epigrams of Jonson have been discovered (49, 68, and 100) variously charging "playwright" (reasonably identified with Marston) with scurrility, cowardice, and plagiarism; though the dates of the epigrams cannot be ascertained with certainty.

Jonson's own statement of the matter to Drummond runs: "He had many quarrels with Marston, beat him, and took his pistol from him, wrote his "Poetaster" on him; the beginning[s] of them were that Marston represented him on the stage."*

*The best account of this whole subject is to be found in the edition of "Poetaster" and "Satiromastrix" by J. H. Penniman in "Belles Lettres Series" shortly to appear. See also his earlier work, "The War of the Theatres," 1892, and the excellent contributions to the subject by H. C. Hart in "Notes and Queries," and in his edition of Jonson, 1906.

Here at least we are on certain ground; and the principals of the quarrel are known. "Histriomastix," a play revised by Marston in 1598, has been regarded as the one in which Jonson was thus "represented on the stage"; although the personage in question, Chrisogonus, a poet, satirist, and translator, poor but proud, and contemptuous of the common herd, seems rather a complimentary portrait of Jonson than a caricature. As to the personages actually ridiculed in "Every Man Out of His Humour," Carlo Buffone was formerly thought certainly to be Marston, as he was described as "a public, scurrilous, and profane jester," and elsewhere as the grand scourge or second untruss [that is, satirist], of the time (Joseph Hall being by his own boast the first, and Marston's work being entitled "The Scourge of Villainy"). Apparently we must now prefer for Carlo a notorious character named Charles Chester, of whom gossipy and inaccurate Aubrey relates that he was "a bold impertinent fellow...a perpetual talker and made a noise like a drum in a room. So one time at a tavern Sir Walter Raleigh beats him and seals up his mouth (that is his upper and nether beard) with hard wax. From him Ben Jonson takes his Carlo Buffone ['i.e.', jester] in "Every Man in His Humour" ['sic']." Is it conceivable that after all Jonson was ridiculing Marston, and that the point of the satire consisted in an intentional confusion of "the grand scourge or second untruss" with "the scurrilous and profane" Chester?

We have digressed into detail in this particular case to exemplify the difficulties of criticism in its attempts to identify the allusions in these forgotten quarrels. We are on sounder ground of fact in recording other manifestations of Jonson's enmity. In "The Case is Altered" there is clear ridicule in the character Antonio Balladino of Anthony Munday, pageant-poet of the city, translator of romances and playwright as well. In "Every Man in His Humour" there is certainly a caricature of Samuel Daniel, accepted poet of the court, sonneteer, and companion of men of fashion. These men held recognised positions to which Jonson felt his talents better entitled him; they were hence to him his natural enemies. It seems almost certain that he pursued both in the personages of his satire through "Every Man Out of His Humour," and "Cynthia's Revels," Daniel under the characters Fastidious Brisk and Hedon, Munday as Puntarvolo and Amorphus; but in these last we venture on quagmire once more. Jonson's literary rivalry of Daniel is traceable again and again, in the entertainments that welcomed King James on his way to London, in the masques at court, and in the pastoral drama. As to Jonson's personal ambitions with respect to these two men, it is notable that he became, not pageant-poet, but chronologer to the City of London; and that, on the accession of the new king, he came soon to triumph over Daniel as the accepted entertainer of royalty.

"Cynthia's Revels," the second "comical satire," was acted in 1600, and, as a play, is even more lengthy, elaborate, and impossible than "Every Man Out of His Humour." Here personal satire seems to have absorbed everything, and while much of the caricature is admirable, especially in the detail of witty and trenchantly satirical dialogue, the central idea of a fountain of self-love is not very well carried out, and the persons revert at times to abstractions, the action to allegory. It adds to our wonder that this difficult drama should have been acted by the Children of Queen Elizabeth's Chapel, among them Nathaniel Field with whom Jonson read Horace and Martial, and whom he taught later how to make plays. Another of these precocious little actors was Salathiel Pavy, who died before he was thirteen, already famed for taking the parts of old men. Him Jonson immortalised in one of the sweetest of his epitaphs. An interesting sidelight is this on the character of this redoubtable and rugged satirist, that he should thus have befriended and tenderly remembered these little theatrical waifs, some of whom (as we know) had been literally kidnapped to be pressed into the service of the theatre and whipped to the conning of their difficult parts. To the caricature of Daniel and Munday in "Cynthia's Revels" must be added Anaides (impudence), here assuredly Marston, and Asotus (the prodigal), interpreted as Lodge or, more perilously, Raleigh. Crites, like Asper-Macilente in "Every Man Out of His Humour," is Jonson's self-complaisant portrait of himself, the just, wholly admirable, and judicious scholar, holding his head high above the pack of the yelping curs of envy and detraction, but careless of their puny attacks on his perfections with only too mindful a neglect.

The third and last of the "comical satires" is "Poetaster," acted, once more, by the Children of the Chapel in 1601, and Jonson's only avowed contribution to the fray. According to the author's own account, this play was written in fifteen weeks on a report that his enemies had entrusted to Dekker the preparation of "Satiromastix, the Untrussing of the Humorous Poet," a dramatic attack upon himself. In this attempt to forestall his enemies Jonson succeeded, and "Poetaster" was an immediate and deserved success. While hardly more closely knit in structure than its earlier companion pieces, "Poetaster" is planned to lead up to the ludicrous final scene in which, after a device borrowed from the "Lexiphanes" of Lucian, the offending poetaster, Marston-Crispinus, is made to throw up the difficult words with which he had overburdened his stomach as well as overlarded his vocabulary. In the end Crispinus with his fellow, Dekker-Demetrius, is bound over to keep the peace and never thenceforward "malign, traduce, or detract the person or writings of Quintus Horatius Flaccus [Jonson] or any other eminent man transcending you in merit." One of the most diverting personages in Jonson's comedy is Captain Tucca. "His peculiarity" has been well described by Ward as "a buoyant blackguardism which recovers itself instantaneously from the most complete exposure, and a picturesqueness of speech like that of a walking dictionary of slang."

It was this character, Captain Tucca, that Dekker hit upon in his reply, "Satiromastix," and he amplified him, turning his abusive vocabulary back upon Jonson and adding "an immodesty to his dialogue that did not enter into Jonson's conception." It has been held, altogether plausibly, that when Dekker was engaged professionally, so to speak, to write a dramatic reply to Jonson, he was at work on a species of chronicle history, dealing with the story of Walter Terill in the reign of William Rufus. This he hurriedly adapted to include the satirical characters suggested by "Poetaster," and fashioned to convey the satire of his reply. The absurdity of placing Horace in the court of a Norman king is the result. But Dekker's play is not without its palpable hits at the arrogance, the literary pride, and self-righteousness of Jonson-Horace, whose "ningle" or pal, the absurd Asinius Bubo, has recently been shown to figure forth, in all likelihood, Jonson's friend, the poet Drayton. Slight and hastily adapted as is "Satiromastix," especially in a comparison with the better wrought and more significant satire of "Poetaster," the town awarded the palm to Dekker, not to Jonson; and Jonson gave over in consequence his practice of "comical satire." Though Jonson was cited to appear before the Lord Chief Justice to answer certain charges to the effect that he had attacked lawyers and soldiers in "Poetaster," nothing came of this complaint. It may be suspected that much of this furious clatter and give-and-take was pure playing to the gallery. The town was agog with the strife, and on no less an authority than Shakespeare ("Hamlet," ii. 2), we learn that the children's company (acting the plays of Jonson) did "so berattle the common stages...that many, wearing rapiers, are afraid of goose-quills, and dare scarce come thither."

Several other plays have been thought to bear a greater or less part in the war of the theatres. Among them the most important is a college play, entitled "The Return from Parnassus," dating 1601-02. In it a much-quoted passage makes Burbage, as a character, declare: "Why here's our fellow Shakespeare puts them all down; aye and Ben Jonson, too. O that Ben Jonson is a pestilent fellow; he brought up Horace, giving the poets a pill, but our fellow Shakespeare hath given him a purge that made him bewray his credit." Was Shakespeare then concerned in this war of the stages? And what could have been the nature of this "purge"? Among several suggestions, "Troilus and Cressida" has been thought by some to be the play in which Shakespeare thus "put down" his friend, Jonson. A wiser interpretation finds the "purge" in "Satiromastix," which, though not written by Shakespeare, was staged by his company, and therefore with his approval and under his direction as one of the leaders of that company.

The last years of the reign of Elizabeth thus saw Jonson recognised as a dramatist second only to Shakespeare, and not second even to him as a dramatic satirist. But Jonson now turned his talents to new fields. Plays on subjects derived from classical story and myth had held the stage from the beginning of the drama, so that Shakespeare was making no new departure when he wrote his "Julius Caesar" about 1600. Therefore when Jonson staged "Sejanus," three years later and with Shakespeare's company once more, he was only following in the elder dramatist's footsteps. But Jonson's idea of a play on classical history, on the one hand, and Shakespeare's and the elder popular dramatists, on the other, were very different. Heywood some years before had put five straggling plays on the stage in quick succession, all derived from stories in Ovid and dramatised with little taste or discrimination. Shakespeare had a finer conception of form, but even he was contented to take all his ancient history from North's translation of Plutarch and dramatise his subject without further inquiry. Jonson was a scholar and a classical antiquarian. He reprobated this slipshod amateurishness, and wrote his "Sejanus" like a scholar, reading Tacitus, Suetonius, and other authorities, to be certain of his facts, his setting, and his atmosphere, and somewhat pedantically noting his authorities in the margin when he came to print. "Sejanus" is a tragedy of genuine dramatic power in which is told with discriminating taste the story of the haughty favourite of Tiberius with his tragical overthrow. Our drama presents no truer nor more painstaking representation of ancient Roman life than may be found in Jonson's "Sejanus" and "Catiline his Conspiracy," which followed in 1611. A passage in the address of the former play to the reader, in which Jonson refers to a collaboration in an earlier version, has led to the surmise that Shakespeare may have been that "worthier pen." There is no evidence to determine the matter.

In 1605, we find Jonson in active collaboration with Chapman and Marston in the admirable comedy of London life entitled "Eastward Hoe." In the previous year, Marston had dedicated his "Malcontent," in terms of fervid admiration, to Jonson; so that the wounds of the war of the theatres must have been long since healed. Between Jonson and Chapman there was the kinship of similar scholarly ideals. The two continued friends throughout life. "Eastward Hoe" achieved the extraordinary popularity represented in a demand for three issues in one year. But this was not due entirely to the merits of the play. In its earliest version a passage which an irritable courtier conceived to be derogatory to his nation, the Scots, sent both Chapman and Jonson to jail; but the matter was soon patched up, for by this time Jonson had influence at court.

With the accession of King James, Jonson began his long and successful career as a writer of masques. He wrote more masques than all his competitors together, and they are of an extraordinary variety and poetic excellence. Jonson did not invent the masque; for such premeditated devices to set and frame, so to speak, a court ball had been known and practised in varying degrees of elaboration long before his time. But Jonson gave dramatic value to the masque, especially in his invention of the antimasque, a comedy or farcical element of relief, entrusted to professional players or dancers. He enhanced, as well, the beauty and dignity of those portions of the masque in which noble lords and ladies took their parts to create, by their gorgeous costumes and artistic grouping and evolutions, a sumptuous show. On the mechanical and scenic side Jonson had an inventive and ingenious partner in Inigo Jones, the royal architect, who more than any one man raised the standard of stage representation in the England of his day. Jonson continued active in the service of the court in the writing of masques and other entertainments far into the reign of King Charles; but, towards the end, a quarrel with Jones embittered his life, and the two testy old men appear to have become not only a constant irritation to each other, but intolerable bores at court. In "Hymenaei," "The Masque of Queens," "Love Freed from Ignorance," "Lovers made Men," "Pleasure Reconciled to Virtue," and many more will be found Jonson's aptitude, his taste, his poetry and inventiveness in these by-forms of the drama; while in "The Masque of Christmas," and "The Gipsies Metamorphosed" especially, is discoverable that power of broad comedy which, at court as well as in the city, was not the least element of Jonson's contemporary popularity.

But Jonson had by no means given up the popular stage when he turned to the amusement of King James. In 1605 "Volpone" was produced, "The Silent Woman" in 1609, "The Alchemist" in the following year. These comedies, with "Bartholomew Fair," 1614, represent Jonson at his height, and for constructive cleverness, character successfully conceived in the manner of caricature, wit and brilliancy of dialogue, they stand alone in English drama. "Volpone, or the Fox," is, in a sense, a transition play from the dramatic satires of the war of the theatres to the purer comedy represented in the plays named above. Its subject is a struggle of wit applied to chicanery; for among its dramatis personae, from the villainous Fox himself, his rascally servant Mosca, Voltore (the vulture), Corbaccio and Corvino (the big and the little raven), to Sir Politic Would-be and the rest, there is scarcely a virtuous character in the play. Question has been raised as to whether a story so forbidding can be considered a comedy, for, although the plot ends in the discomfiture and imprisonment of the most vicious, it involves no mortal catastrophe. But Jonson was on sound historical ground, for "Volpone" is conceived far more logically on the lines of the ancients' theory of comedy than was ever the romantic drama of Shakespeare, however repulsive we may find a philosophy of life that facilely divides the world into the rogues and their dupes, and, identifying brains with roguery and innocence with folly, admires the former while inconsistently punishing them.

"The Silent Woman" is a gigantic farce of the most ingenious construction. The whole comedy hinges on a huge joke, played by a heartless nephew on his misanthropic uncle, who is induced to take to himself a wife, young, fair, and warranted silent, but who, in the end, turns out neither silent nor a woman at all. In "The Alchemist," again, we have the utmost cleverness in construction, the whole fabric building climax on climax, witty, ingenious, and so plausibly presented that we forget its departures from the possibilities of life. In "The Alchemist" Jonson represented, none the less to the life, certain sharpers of the metropolis, revelling in their shrewdness and rascality and in the variety of the stupidity and wickedness of their victims. We may object to the fact that the only person in the play possessed of a scruple of honesty is discomfited, and that the greatest scoundrel of all is approved in the end and rewarded. The comedy is so admirably written and contrived, the personages stand out with such lifelike distinctness in their several kinds, and the whole is animated with such verve and resourcefulness that "The Alchemist" is a new marvel every time it is read. Lastly of this group comes the tremendous comedy, "Bartholomew Fair," less clear cut, less definite, and less structurally worthy of praise than its three predecessors, but full of the keenest and cleverest of satire and inventive to a degree beyond any English comedy save some other of Jonson's own. It is in "Bartholomew Fair" that we are presented to the immortal caricature of the Puritan, Zeal-in-the-Land Busy, and the Littlewits that group about him, and it is in this extraordinary comedy that the humour of Jonson, always open to this danger, loosens into the Rabelaisian mode that so delighted King James in "The Gipsies Metamorphosed." Another comedy of less merit is "The Devil is an Ass," acted in 1616. It was the failure of this play that caused Jonson to give over writing for the public stage for a period of nearly ten years.

"Volpone" was laid as to scene in Venice. Whether because of the success of "Eastward Hoe" or for other reasons, the other three comedies declare in the words of the prologue to "The Alchemist":

"Our scene is London, 'cause we would make known No country's mirth is better than our own."

Indeed Jonson went further when he came to revise his plays for collected publication in his folio of 1616, he transferred the scene of "Every Man in His Humour" from Florence to London also, converting Signior Lorenzo di Pazzi to Old Kno'well, Prospero to Master Welborn, and Hesperida to Dame Kitely "dwelling i' the Old Jewry."

In his comedies of London life, despite his trend towards caricature, Jonson has shown himself a genuine realist, drawing from the life about him with an experience and insight rare in any generation. A happy comparison has been suggested between Ben Jonson and Charles Dickens. Both were men of the people, lowly born and hardly bred. Each knew the London of his time as few men knew it; and each represented it intimately and in elaborate detail. Both men were at heart moralists, seeking the truth by the exaggerated methods of humour and caricature; perverse, even wrong-headed at times, but possessed of a true pathos and largeness of heart, and when all has been said -- though the Elizabethan ran to satire, the Victorian to sentimentality -- leaving the world better for the art that they practised in it.

In 1616, the year of the death of Shakespeare, Jonson collected his plays, his poetry, and his masques for publication in a collective edition. This was an unusual thing at the time and had been attempted by no dramatist before Jonson. This volume published, in a carefully revised text, all the plays thus far mentioned, excepting "The Case is Altered," which Jonson did not acknowledge, "Bartholomew Fair," and "The Devil is an Ass," which was written too late. It included likewise a book of some hundred and thirty odd "Epigrams," in which form of brief and pungent writing Jonson was an acknowledged master; "The Forest," a smaller collection of lyric and occasional verse and some ten "Masques" and "Entertainments." In this same year Jonson was made poet laureate with a pension of one hundred marks a year. This, with his fees and returns from several noblemen, and the small earnings of his plays must have formed the bulk of his income. The poet appears to have done certain literary hack-work for others, as, for example, parts of the Punic Wars contributed to Raleigh's "History of the World." We know from a story, little to the credit of either, that Jonson accompanied Raleigh's son abroad in the capacity of a tutor. In 1618 Jonson was granted the reversion of the office of Master of the Revels, a post for which he was peculiarly fitted; but he did not live to enjoy its perquisites. Jonson was honoured with degrees by both universities, though when and under what circumstances is not known. It has been said that he narrowly escaped the honour of knighthood, which the satirists of the day averred King James was wont to lavish with an indiscriminate hand. Worse men were made knights in his day than worthy Ben Jonson.

From 1616 to the close of the reign of King James, Jonson produced nothing for the stage. But he "prosecuted" what he calls "his wonted studies" with such assiduity that he became in reality, as by report, one of the most learned men of his time. Jonson's theory of authorship involved a wide acquaintance with books and "an ability," as he put it, "to convert the substance or riches of another poet to his own use." Accordingly Jonson read not only the Greek and Latin classics down to the lesser writers, but he acquainted himself especially with the Latin writings of his learned contemporaries, their prose as well as their poetry, their antiquities and curious lore as well as their more solid learning. Though a poor man, Jonson was an indefatigable collector of books. He told Drummond that "the Earl of Pembroke sent him 20 pounds every first day of the new year to buy new books." Unhappily, in 1623, his library was destroyed by fire, an accident serio-comically described in his witty poem, "An Execration upon Vulcan." Yet even now a book turns up from time to time in which is inscribed, in fair large Italian lettering, the name, Ben Jonson. With respect to Jonson's use of his material, Dryden said memorably of him: "He was not only a professed imitator of Horace, but a learned plagiary of all the others; you track him everywhere in their snow....But he has done his robberies so openly that one sees he fears not to be taxed by any law. He invades authors like a monarch, and what would be theft in other poets is only victory in him." And yet it is but fair to say that Jonson prided himself, and justly, on his originality. In "Catiline," he not only uses Sallust's account of the conspiracy, but he models some of the speeches of Cicero on the Roman orator's actual words. In "Poetaster," he lifts a whole satire out of Horace and dramatises it effectively for his purposes. The sophist Libanius suggests the situation of "The Silent Woman"; a Latin comedy of Giordano Bruno, "Il Candelaio," the relation of the dupes and the sharpers in "The Alchemist," the "Mostellaria" of Plautus, its admirable opening scene. But Jonson commonly bettered his sources, and putting the stamp of his sovereignty on whatever bullion he borrowed made it thenceforward to all time current and his own.

The lyric and especially the occasional poetry of Jonson has a peculiar merit. His theory demanded design and the perfection of literary finish. He was furthest from the rhapsodist and the careless singer of an idle day; and he believed that Apollo could only be worthily served in singing robes and laurel crowned. And yet many of Jonson's lyrics will live as long as the language. Who does not know "Queen and huntress, chaste and fair." "Drink to me only with thine eyes," or "Still to be neat, still to be dressed"? Beautiful in form, deft and graceful in expression, with not a word too much or one that bears not its part in the total effect, there is yet about the lyrics of Jonson a certain stiffness and formality, a suspicion that they were not quite spontaneous and unbidden, but that they were carved, so to speak, with disproportionate labour by a potent man of letters whose habitual thought is on greater things. It is for these reasons that Jonson is even better in the epigram and in occasional verse where rhetorical finish and pointed wit less interfere with the spontaneity and emotion which we usually associate with lyrical poetry. There are no such epitaphs as Ben Jonson's, witness the charming ones on his own children, on Salathiel Pavy, the child-actor, and many more; and this even though the rigid law of mine and thine must now restore to William Browne of Tavistock the famous lines beginning: "Underneath this sable hearse." Jonson is unsurpassed, too, in the difficult poetry of compliment, seldom falling into fulsome praise and disproportionate similitude, yet showing again and again a generous appreciation of worth in others, a discriminating taste and a generous personal regard. There was no man in England of his rank so well known and universally beloved as Ben Jonson. The list of his friends, of those to whom he had written verses, and those who had written verses to him, includes the name of every man of prominence in the England of King James. And the tone of many of these productions discloses an affectionate familiarity that speaks for the amiable personality and sound worth of the laureate. In 1619, growing unwieldy through inactivity, Jonson hit upon the heroic remedy of a journey afoot to Scotland. On his way thither and back he was hospitably received at the houses of many friends and by those to whom his friends had recommended him. When he arrived in Edinburgh, the burgesses met to grant him the freedom of the city, and Drummond, foremost of Scottish poets, was proud to entertain him for weeks as his guest at Hawthornden. Some of the noblest of Jonson's poems were inspired by friendship. Such is the fine "Ode to the memory of Sir Lucius Cary and Sir Henry Moryson," and that admirable piece of critical insight and filial affection, prefixed to the first Shakespeare folio, "To the memory of my beloved master, William Shakespeare, and what he hath left us," to mention only these. Nor can the earlier "Epode," beginning "Not to know vice at all," be matched in stately gravity and gnomic wisdom in its own wise and stately age.

But if Jonson had deserted the stage after the publication of his folio and up to the end of the reign of King James, he was far from inactive; for year after year his inexhaustible inventiveness continued to contribute to the masquing and entertainment at court. In "The Golden Age Restored," Pallas turns the Iron Age with its attendant evils into statues which sink out of sight; in "Pleasure Reconciled to Virtue," Atlas figures represented as an old man, his shoulders covered with snow, and Comus, "the god of cheer or the belly," is one of the characters, a circumstance which an imaginative boy of ten, named John Milton, was not to forget. "Pan's Anniversary," late in the reign of James, proclaimed that Jonson had not yet forgotten how to write exquisite lyrics, and "The Gipsies Metamorphosed" displayed the old drollery and broad humorous stroke still unimpaired and unmatchable. These, too, and the earlier years of Charles were the days of the Apollo Room of the Devil Tavern where Jonson presided, the absolute monarch of English literary Bohemia. We hear of a room blazoned about with Jonson's own judicious "Leges Convivales" in letters of gold, of a company made up of the choicest spirits of the time, devotedly attached to their veteran dictator, his reminiscences, opinions, affections, and enmities. And we hear, too, of valorous potations; but in the words of Herrick addressed to his master, Jonson, at the Devil Tavern, as at the Dog, the Triple Tun, and at the Mermaid,

"We such clusters had
As made us nobly wild, not mad,
And yet each verse of thine
Outdid the meat, outdid the frolic wine."

But the patronage of the court failed in the days of King Charles, though Jonson was not without royal favours; and the old poet returned to the stage, producing, between 1625 and 1633, "The Staple of News," "The New Inn," "The Magnetic Lady," and "The Tale of a Tub," the last doubtless revised from a much earlier comedy. None of these plays met with any marked success, although the scathing generalisation of Dryden that designated them "Jonson's dotages" is unfair to their genuine merits. Thus the idea of an office for the gathering, proper dressing, and promulgation of news (wild flight of the fancy in its time) was an excellent subject for satire on the existing absurdities among newsmongers; although as much can hardly be said for "The Magnetic Lady," who, in her bounty, draws to her personages of differing humours to reconcile them in the end according to the alternative title, or "Humours Reconciled." These last plays of the old dramatist revert to caricature and the hard lines of allegory; the moralist is more than ever present, the satire degenerates into personal lampoon, especially of his sometime friend, Inigo Jones, who appears unworthily to have used his influence at court against the broken-down old poet. And now disease claimed Jonson, and he was bedridden for months. He had succeeded Middleton in 1628 as Chronologer to the City of London, but lost the post for not fulfilling its duties. King Charles befriended him, and even commissioned him to write still for the entertainment of the court; and he was not without the sustaining hand of noble patrons and devoted friends among the younger poets who were proud to be "sealed of the tribe of Ben."

Jonson died, August 6, 1637, and a second folio of his works, which he had been some time gathering, was printed in 1640, bearing in its various parts dates ranging from 1630 to 1642. It included all the plays mentioned in the foregoing paragraphs, excepting "The Case is Altered;" the masques, some fifteen, that date between 1617 and 1630; another collection of lyrics and occasional poetry called "Underwoods", including some further entertainments; a translation of "Horace's Art of Poetry" (also published in a vicesimo quarto in 1640), and certain fragments and ingatherings which the poet would hardly have included himself. These last comprise the fragment (less than seventy lines) of a tragedy called "Mortimer his Fall," and three acts of a pastoral drama of much beauty and poetic spirit, "The Sad Shepherd." There is also the exceedingly interesting "English Grammar" "made by Ben Jonson for the benefit of all strangers out of his observation of the English language now spoken and in use," in Latin and English; and "Timber, or Discoveries" "made upon men and matter as they have flowed out of his daily reading, or had their reflux to his peculiar notion of the times." The "Discoveries," as it is usually called, is a commonplace book such as many literary men have kept, in which their reading was chronicled, passages that took their fancy translated or transcribed, and their passing opinions noted. Many passages of Jonson's "Discoveries" are literal translations from the authors he chanced to be reading, with the reference, noted or not, as the accident of the moment prescribed. At times he follows the line of

Macchiavelli's argument as to the nature and conduct of princes; at others he clarifies his own conception of poetry and poets by recourse to Aristotle. He finds a choice paragraph on eloquence in Seneca the elder and applies it to his own recollection of Bacon's power as an orator; and another on facile and ready genius, and translates it, adapting it to his recollection of his fellow-playwright, Shakespeare. To call such passages -- which Jonson never intended for publication -- plagiarism, is to obscure the significance of words. To disparage his memory by citing them is a preposterous use of scholarship. Jonson's prose, both in his dramas, in the descriptive comments of his masques, and in the "Discoveries," is characterised by clarity and vigorous directness, nor is it wanting in a fine sense of form or in the subtler graces of diction.

When Jonson died there was a project for a handsome monument to his memory. But the Civil War was at hand, and the project failed. A memorial, not insufficient, was carved on the stone covering his grave in one of the aisles of Westminster Abbey:

"O rare Ben Jonson."

Felix E. Schelling

A Glossary of Words & Meanings

In this modern day words and their meanings have evolved through many forms. Listed below are words commonly used by Jonson and his contemporaries and the meanings attributed to them then.

ABATE, cast down, subdue.

ABHORRING, repugnant (to), at variance.

ABJECT, base, degraded thing, outcast.

ABRASE, smooth, blank.

ABSOLUTE(LY), faultless(ly).

ABSTRACTED, abstract, abstruse.

ABUSE, deceive, insult, dishonour, make ill use of.

ACATER, caterer.

ACATES, cates.

ACCEPTIVE, willing, ready to accept, receive.

ACCOMMODATE, fit, befitting. (The word was a fashionable one and used on all occasions. See "Henry IV.," pt. 2, iii. 4).

ACCOST, draw near, approach.

ACKNOWN, confessedly acquainted with.

ACME, full maturity.

ADALANTADO, lord deputy or governor of a Spanish province.

ADJECTION, addition.

ADMIRATION, astonishment.

ADMIRE, wonder, wonder at.

ADROP, philosopher's stone, or substance from which obtained.

ADSCRIVE, subscribe.

ADULTERATE, spurious, counterfeit.

ADVANCE, lift.

ADVERTISE, inform, give intelligence.

ADVERTISED, "be—," be it known to you.

ADVERTISEMENT, intelligence.

ADVISE, consider, bethink oneself, deliberate.

ADVISED, informed, aware; "are you—?" have you found that out?

AFFECT, love, like; aim at; move.

AFFECTED, disposed; beloved.

AFFECTIONATE, obstinate; prejudiced.

AFFECTS, affections.

AFFRONT, "give the—," face.

AFFY, have confidence in; betroth.

AFTER, after the manner of.

AGAIN, AGAINST, In anticipation of.

AGGRAVATE, increase, magnify, enlarge upon.

AGNOMINATION. See Paranomasie.

AIERY, nest, brood.

AIM, guess.

ALL HID, children's cry at hide-and-seek.

ALL-TO, completely, entirely ("all-to-be-laden").

ALLOWANCE, approbation, recognition.

ALMA-CANTARAS (astronomy), parallels of altitude.

ALMAIN, name of a dance.

ALMUTEN, planet of chief influence in the horoscope.

ALONE, unequalled, without peer.

ALUDELS, subliming pots.

AMAZED, confused, perplexed.

AMBER, AMBRE, ambergris.

AMBREE, MARY, a woman noted for her valour at the siege of Ghent, 1458.

AMES-ACE, lowest throw at dice.

AMPHIBOLIES, ambiguities.

AMUSED, bewildered, amazed.

AN, if.

ANATOMY, skeleton, or dissected body.

ANDIRONS, fire-dogs.

ANGEL, gold coin worth 10 shillings, stamped with the figure of the archangel Michael.

ANNESH CLEARE, spring known as Agnes le Clare.

ANSWER, return hit in fencing.

ANTIC, ANTIQUE, clown, buffoon.

ANTIC, like a buffoon.

ANTIPERISTASIS, an opposition which enhances the quality it opposes.

APOZEM, decoction.

APPERIL, peril.

APPLE-JOHN, APPLE-SQUIRE, pimp, pander.

APPLY, attach.

APPREHEND, take into custody.

APPREHENSIVE, quick of perception; able to perceive and appreciate.

APPROVE, prove, confirm.

APT, suit, adapt; train, prepare; dispose, incline.

APT(LY), suitable(y), opportune(ly).

APTITUDE, suitableness.

ARBOR, "make the—," cut up the game (Gifford).

ARCHES, Court of Arches.

ARCHIE, Archibald Armstrong, jester to James I. and Charles I.

ARGAILE, argol, crust or sediment in wine casks.

ARGENT-VIVE, quicksilver.

ARGUMENT, plot of a drama; theme, subject; matter in question; token, proof.

ARRIDE, please.

ARSEDINE, mixture of copper and zinc, used as an imitation of gold-leaf.

ARTHUR, PRINCE, reference to an archery show by a society who assumed arms, etc., of Arthur's knights.

ARTICLE, item.

ARTIFICIALLY, artfully.

ASCENSION, evaporation, distillation.

ASPIRE, try to reach, obtain, long for.

ASSALTO (Italian), assault.

ASSAY, draw a knife along the belly of the deer, a ceremony of the hunting-field.

ASSOIL, solve.

ASSURE, secure possession or reversion of.

ATHANOR, a digesting furnace, calculated to keep up a constant heat.

ATONE, reconcile.

ATTACH, attack, seize.

AUDACIOUS, having spirit and confidence.

AUTHENTIC(AL), of authority, authorised, trustworthy, genuine.

AVISEMENT, reflection, consideration.

AVOID, begone! get rid of.

AWAY WITH, endure.

AZOCH, Mercurius Philosophorum.

BABION, baboon.

BABY, doll.

BACK-SIDE, back premises.

BAFFLE, treat with contempt.

BAGATINE, Italian coin, worth about the third of a farthing.

BAIARD, horse of magic powers known to old romance.

BALDRICK, belt worn across the breast to support bugle, etc.

BALE (of dice), pair.

BALK, overlook, pass by, avoid.

BALLACE, ballast.

BALLOO, game at ball.

BALNEUM (BAIN MARIE), a vessel for holding hot water in which other vessels are stood for heating.

BANBURY, "brother of—," Puritan.

BANDOG, dog tied or chained up.

BANE, woe, ruin.

BANQUET, a light repast; dessert.

BARB, to clip gold.

BARBEL, fresh-water fish.

BARE, meer; bareheaded; it was "a particular mark of state and grandeur for the coachman to be uncovered" (Gifford).

BARLEY-BREAK, game somewhat similar to base.

BASE, game of prisoner's base.

BASES, richly embroidered skirt reaching to the knees, or lower.

BASILISK, fabulous reptile, believed to slay with its eye.

BASKET, used for the broken provision collected for prisoners.

BASON, basons, etc., were beaten by the attendant mob when bad characters were "carted."

BATE, be reduced; abate, reduce.

BATOON, baton, stick.

BATTEN, feed, grow fat.

BAWSON, badger.

BEADSMAN, prayer-man, one engaged to pray for another.

BEAGLE, small hound; fig. spy.

BEAR IN HAND, keep in suspense, deceive with false hopes.

BEARWARD, bear leader.

BEDPHERE. See Phere.

BEDSTAFF, (?) wooden pin in the side of the bedstead for supporting the bedclothes (Johnson); one of the sticks or "laths"; a stick used in making a bed.

BEETLE, heavy mallet.

BEG, "I'd—him," the custody of minors and idiots was begged for; likewise property fallen forfeit to the Crown ("your house had been begged").

BELL-MAN, night watchman.

BENJAMIN, an aromatic gum.

BERLINA, pillory.

BESCUMBER, defile.

BESLAVE, beslabber.

BESOGNO, beggar.

BESPAWLE, bespatter.

BETHLEHEM GABOR, Transylvanian hero, proclaimed King of Hungary.

BEVER, drinking.

BEVIS, SIR, knight of romance whose horse was equally celebrated.

BEWRAY, reveal, make known.

BEZANT, heraldic term: small gold circle.

BEZOAR'S STONE, a remedy known by this name was a supposed antidote to poison.

BID-STAND, highwayman.

BIGGIN, cap, similar to that worn by the Beguines; nightcap.

BILIVE (belive), with haste.

BILK, nothing, empty talk.

BILL, kind of pike.

BILLET, wood cut for fuel, stick.

BIRDING, thieving.

BLACK SANCTUS, burlesque hymn, any unholy riot.

BLANK, originally a small French coin.

BLANK, white.

BLANKET, toss in a blanket.

BLAZE, outburst of violence.

BLAZE, (her.) blazon; publish abroad.

BLAZON, armorial bearings; fig. all that pertains to good birth and breeding.

BLIN, "withouten—," without ceasing.

BLOW, puff up.

BLUE, colour of servants' livery, hence "—order," "—waiters."

BLUSHET, blushing one.

BOB, jest, taunt.

BOB, beat, thump.

BODGE, measure.

BODKIN, dagger, or other short, pointed weapon; long pin with which the women fastened up their hair.

BOLT, roll (of material).

BOLT, dislodge, rout out; sift (boulting-tub).

BOLT'S-HEAD, long, straight-necked vessel for distillation.

BOMBARD SLOPS, padded, puffed-out breeches.

BONA ROBA, "good, wholesome, plum-cheeked wench" (Johnson) —not always used in compliment.

BONNY-CLABBER, sour butter-milk.

BOOKHOLDER, prompter.

BOOT, "to—," into the bargain; "no—," of no avail.

BORACHIO, bottle made of skin.

BORDELLO, brothel.

BORNE IT, conducted, carried it through.

BOTTLE (of hay), bundle, truss.

BOI IOM, skein or ball of thread; vessel.

BOURD, jest.

BOVOLI, snails or cockles dressed in the Italian manner (Gifford).

BOW-POT, flower vase or pot.

BOYS, "terrible—," "angry—," roystering young bucks. (See Nares).

BRABBLES (BRABBLESH), brawls.

BRACH, bitch.

BRADAMANTE, a heroine in "Orlando Furioso."

BRADLEY, ARTHUR OF, a lively character commemorated in ballads.

BRAKE, frame for confining a horse's feet while being shod, or strong curb or bridle; trap.

BRANCHED, with "detached sleeve ornaments, projecting from the shoulders of the gown" (Gifford).

BRANDISH, flourish of weapon.

BRASH, brace.

BRAVE, bravado, braggart speech.

BRAVE (adv.), gaily, finely (apparelled).

BRAVERIES, gallants.

BRAVERY, extravagant gaiety of apparel.

BRAVO, bravado, swaggerer.

BRAZEN-HEAD, speaking head made by Roger Bacon.

BREATHE, pause for relaxation; exercise.

BREATH UPON, speak dispraisingly of.

BREND, burn.

BRIDE-ALE, wedding feast.

BRIEF, abstract; (mus.) breve.

BRISK, smartly dressed.

BRIZE, breese, gadfly.

BROAD-SEAL, state seal.

BROCK, badger (term of contempt).

BROKE, transact business as a broker.

BROOK, endure, put up with.

BROUGHTON, HUGH, an English divine and Hebrew scholar.

BRUIT, rumour.

BUCK, wash.

BUCKLE, bend.

BUFF, leather made of buffalo skin, used for military and serjeants' coats, etc.

BUFO, black tincture.

BUGLE, long-shaped bead.

BULLED, (?) bolled, swelled.

BULLIONS, trunk hose.

BULLY, term of familiar endearment.

BUNGY, Friar Bungay, who had a familiar in the shape of a dog.

BURDEN, refrain, chorus.

BURGONET, closely-fitting helmet with visor.

BURGULLION, braggadocio.

BURN, mark wooden measures ("—ing of cans").

BURROUGH, pledge, security.

BUSKIN, half-boot, foot gear reaching high up the leg.

BUTT-SHAFT, barbless arrow for shooting at butts.

BUTTER, NATHANIEL ("Staple of News"), a compiler of general news. (See Cunningham).

BUTTERY-HATCH, half-door shutting off the buttery, where provisions and liquors were stored.

BUY, "he bought me," formerly the guardianship of wards could be bought.

BUZ, exclamation to enjoin silence.

BUZZARD, simpleton.

BY AND BY, at once.

BY(E), "on the __," incidentally, as of minor or secondary importance; at the side.

BY-CHOP, by-blow, bastard.

CADUCEUS, Mercury's wand.

CALIVER, light kind of musket.

CALLET, woman of ill repute.

CALLOT, coif worn on the wigs of our judges or serjeants-at-law (Gifford).

CALVERED, crimped, or sliced and pickled. (See Nares).

CAMOUCCIO, wretch, knave.

CAMUSED, flat.

CAN, knows.

CANDLE-RENT, rent from house property.

CANDLE-WASTER, one who studies late.

CANTER, sturdy beggar.

CAP OF MAINTENCE, an insignia of dignity, a cap of state borne before kings at their coronation; also an heraldic term.

CAPABLE, able to comprehend, fit to receive instruction, impression.

CAPANEUS, one of the "Seven against Thebes."

CARACT, carat, unit of weight for precious stones, etc.; value, worth.

CARANZA, Spanish author of a book on duelling.

CARCANET, jewelled ornament for the neck.

CARE, take care; object.

CAROSH, coach, carriage.

CARPET, table-cover.

CARRIAGE, bearing, behaviour.

CARWHITCHET, quip, pun.

CASAMATE, casemate, fortress.

CASE, a pair.

CASE, "in—," in condition.

CASSOCK, soldier's loose overcoat.

CAST, flight of hawks, couple.

CAST, throw dice; vomit; forecast, calculate.

CAST, cashiered.

CASTING-GLASS, bottle for sprinkling perfume.

CASTRIL, kestrel, falcon.

CAT, structure used in sieges.

CATAMITE, old form of "ganymede."

CATASTROPHE, conclusion.

CATCHPOLE, sheriff's officer.

CATES, dainties, provisions.

CATSO, rogue, cheat.

CAUTELOUS, crafty, artful.

CENSURE, criticism; sentence.

CENSURE, criticise; pass sentence, doom.

CERUSE, cosmetic containing white lead.

CESS, assess.

CHANGE, "hunt—," follow a fresh scent.

CHAPMAN, retail dealer.

CHARACTER, handwriting.

CHARGE, expense.

CHARM, subdue with magic, lay a spell on, silence.

CHARMING, exercising magic power.

CHARTEL, challenge.

CHEAP, bargain, market.

CHEAR, CHEER, comfort, encouragement; food, entertainment.

CHECK AT, aim reproof at.

CHEQUIN, gold Italian coin.

CHEVRIL, from kidskin, which is elastic and pliable.

CHIAUS, Turkish envoy; used for a cheat, swindler.

CHILDERMASS DAY, Innocents' Day.

CHOKE-BAIL, action which does not allow of bail.

CHRYSOPOEIA, alchemy.

CHRYSOSPERM, ways of producing gold.

CIBATION, adding fresh substances to supply the waste of evaporation.

CIMICI, bugs.

CINOPER, cinnabar.

CIOPPINI, chopine, lady's high shoe.

CIRCLING BOY, "a species of roarer; one who in some way drew a man into a snare, to cheat or rob him" (Nares).

CIRCUMSTANCE, circumlocution, beating about the bush; ceremony, everything pertaining to a certain condition; detail, particular.

CITRONISE, turn citron colour.

CITTERN, kind of guitar.

CITY-WIRES, woman of fashion, who made use of wires for hair and dress.

CIVIL, legal.

CLAP, clack, chatter.

CLAPPER-DUDGEON, downright beggar.

CLAPS HIS DISH, a clap, or clack, dish (dish with a movable lid) was carried by beggars and lepers to show that the vessel was empty, and to give sound of their approach.

CLARIDIANA, heroine of an old romance.

CLARISSIMO, Venetian noble.

CLEM, starve.

CLICKET, latch.

CLIM O' THE CLOUGHS, etc., wordy heroes of romance.

CLIMATE, country.

CLOSE, secret, private; secretive.

CLOSENESS, secrecy.

CLOTH, arras, hangings.

CLOUT, mark shot at, bull's eye.

CLOWN, countryman, clodhopper.

COACH-LEAVES, folding blinds.

COALS, "bear no—," submit to no affront.

COAT-ARMOUR, coat of arms.

COAT-CARD, court-card.

COB-HERRING, HERRING-COB, a young herring.

COB-SWAN, male swan.

COCK-A-HOOP, denoting unstinted jollity; thought to be derived from turning on the tap that all might drink to the full of the flowing liquor.

COCKATRICE, reptile supposed to be produced from a cock's egg and to kill by its eye—used as a term of reproach for a woman.

COCK-BRAINED, giddy, wild.

COCKER, pamper.

COCKSCOMB, fool's cap.

COCKSTONE, stone said to be found in a cock's gizzard, and to possess particular virtues.

CODLING, softening by boiling.

COFFIN, raised crust of a pie.

COG, cheat, wheedle.

COIL, turmoil, confusion, ado.

COKELY, master of a puppet-show (Whalley).

COKES, fool, gull.

COLD-CONCEITED, having cold opinion of, coldly affected towards.

COLE-HARBOUR, a retreat for people of all sorts.

COLLECTION, composure; deduction.

COLLOP, small slice, piece of flesh.

COLLY, blacken.

COLOUR, pretext.

COLOURS, "fear no—," no enemy (quibble).

COLSTAFF, cowlstaff, pole for carrying a cowl=tub.

COME ABOUT, charge, turn round.

COMFORTABLE BREAD, spiced gingerbread.

COMING, forward, ready to respond, complaisant.

COMMENT, commentary; "sometime it is taken for a lie or fayned tale" (Bullokar, 1616).

COMMODITY, "current for—," allusion to practice of money-lenders, who forced the borrower to take part of the loan in the shape of worthless goods on which the latter had to make money if he could.

COMMUNICATE, share.

COMPASS, "in—," within the range, sphere.

COMPLEMENT, completion, completement; anything required for the perfecting or carrying out of a person or affair; accomplishment.

COMPLEXION, natural disposition, constitution.

COMPLIMENT, See Complement.

COMPLIMENTARIES, masters of accomplishments.

COMPOSITION, constitution; agreement, contract.

COMPOSURE, composition.

COMPTER, COUNTER, debtors' prison.

CONCEALMENT, a certain amount of church property had been retained at the dissolution of the monasteries; Elizabeth sent commissioners to search it out, and the courtiers begged for it.

CONCEIT, idea, fancy, witty invention, conception, opinion.

CONCEIT, apprehend.

CONCEITED, fancifully, ingeniously devised or conceived; possessed of intelligence, witty, ingenious (hence well conceited, etc.); disposed to joke; of opinion, possessed of an idea.

CONCEIVE, understand.

CONCENT, harmony, agreement.

CONCLUDE, infer, prove.

CONCOCT, assimilate, digest.

CONDEN'T, probably conducted.

CONDUCT, escort, conductor.

CONEY-CATCH, cheat.

CONFECT, sweetmeat.

CONFER, compare.

CONGIES, bows.

CONNIVE, give a look, wink, of secret intelligence.

CONSORT, company, concert.

CONSTANCY, fidelity, ardour, persistence.

CONSTANT, confirmed, persistent, faithful.

CONSTANTLY, firmly, persistently.

CONTEND, strive.

CONTINENT, holding together.

CONTROL (the point), bear or beat down.

CONVENT, assembly, meeting.

CONVERT, turn (oneself).

CONVEY, transmit from one to another.

CONVINCE, evince, prove; overcome, overpower; convict.

COP, head, top; tuft on head of birds; "a cop" may have reference to one or other meaning; Gifford and others interpret as "conical, terminating in a point."

COPE-MAN, chapman.

COPESMATE, companion.

COPY (Lat. copia), abundance, copiousness.

CORN ("powder—"), grain.

COROLLARY, finishing part or touch.

CORSIVE, corrosive.

CORTINE, curtain, (arch.) wall between two towers, etc.

CORYAT, famous for his travels, published as "Coryat's Crudities."

COSSET, pet lamb, pet.

COSTARD, head.

COSTARD-MONGER, apple-seller, coster-monger.

COSTS, ribs.

COTE, hut.

COTHURNAL, from "cothurnus," a particular boot worn by actors in Greek tragedy.

COTQUEAN, hussy.

COUNSEL, secret.

COUNTENANCE, means necessary for support; credit, standing.

COUNTER. See Compter.

COUNTER, pieces of metal or ivory for calculating at play.

COUNTER, "hunt—," follow scent in reverse direction.

COUNTERFEIT, false coin.

COUNTERPANE, one part or counterpart of a deed or indenture.

COUNTERPOINT, opposite, contrary point.

COURT-DISH, a kind of drinking-cup (Halliwell); N.E.D. quotes from Bp. Goodman's "Court of James I.": "The king... caused his carver to cut him out a court-dish, that is, something of every dish, which he sent him as part of his reversion," but this does not sound like short allowance or small receptacle.

COURT-DOR, fool.

COURTEAU, curtal, small horse with docked tail.

COURTSHIP, courtliness.

COVETISE, avarice.

COWSHARD, cow dung.

COXCOMB, fool's cap, fool.

COY, shrink; disdain.

COYSTREL, low varlet.

COZEN, cheat.

CRACK, lively young rogue, wag.

CRACK, crack up, boast; come to grief.

CRAMBE, game of crambo, in which the players find rhymes for a given word.

CRANCH, craunch.

CRANION, spider-like; also fairy appellation for a fly (Gifford, who refers to lines in Drayton's "Nimphidia").

CRIMP, game at cards.

CRINCLE, draw back, turn aside.

CRISPED, with curled or waved hair.

CROP, gather, reap.

CROPSHIRE, a kind of herring. (See N.E.D.)

CROSS, any piece of money, many coins being stamped with a cross.

CROSS AND PILE, heads and tails.

CROSSLET, crucible.

CROWD, fiddle.

CRUDITIES, undigested matter.

CRUMP, curl up.

CRUSADO, Portuguese gold coin, marked with a cross.

CRY ("he that cried Italian"), "speak in a musical cadence," intone, or declaim (?); cry up.

CUCKING-STOOL, used for the ducking of scolds, etc.

CUCURBITE, a gourd-shaped vessel used for distillation.

CUERPO, "in—," in undress.

CULLICE, broth.

CULLION, base fellow, coward.

CULLISEN, badge worn on their arm by servants.

CULVERIN, kind of cannon.

CUNNING, skill.

CUNNING, skilful.

CUNNING-MAN, fortune-teller.

CURE, care for.

CURIOUS(LY), scrupulous, particular; elaborate, elegant(ly), dainty(ly) (hence "in curious").

CURST, shrewish, mischievous.

CURTAL, dog with docked tail, of inferior sort.

CUSTARD, "quaking—," "—politic," reference to a large custard which formed part of a city feast and afforded huge entertainment, for the fool jumped into it, and other like tricks were played. (See "All's Well, etc." ii. 5, 40.)

CUTWORK, embroidery, open-work.

CYPRES (CYPRUS) (quibble), cypress (or cyprus) being a transparent material, and when black used for mourning.

DAGGER ("—frumety"), name of tavern.

DARGISON, apparently some person known in ballad or tale.

DAUPHIN MY BOY, refrain of old comic song.

DAW, daunt.

DEAD LIFT, desperate emergency.

DEAR, applied to that which in any way touches us nearly.

DECLINE, turn off from; turn away, aside.

DEFALK, deduct, abate.

DEFEND, forbid.

DEGENEROUS, degenerate.

DEGREES, steps.

DELATE, accuse.

DEMI-CULVERIN, cannon carrying a ball of about ten pounds.

DENIER, the smallest possible coin, being the twelfth part of a sou.

DEPART, part with.

DEPENDANCE, ground of quarrel in duello language.

DESERT, reward.

DESIGNMENT, design.

DESPERATE, rash, reckless.

DETECT, allow to be detected, betray, inform against.

DETERMINE, terminate.

DETRACT, draw back, refuse.

DEVICE, masque, show; a thing moved by wires, etc., puppet.

DEVISE, exact in every particular.

DEVISED, invented.

DIAPASM, powdered aromatic herbs, made into balls of perfumed paste. (See Pomander.)

DIBBLE, (?) moustache (N.E.D.); (?) dagger (Cunningham).

DIFFUSED, disordered, scattered, irregular.

DIGHT, dressed.

DILDO, refrain of popular songs; vague term of low meaning.

DIMBLE, dingle, ravine.

DIMENSUM, stated allowance.

DISBASE, debase.

DISCERN, distinguish, show a difference between.

DISCHARGE, settle for.

DISCIPLINE, reformation; ecclesiastical system.

DISCLAIM, renounce all part in.

DISCOURSE, process of reasoning, reasoning faculty.

DISCOURTSHIP, discourtesy.

DISCOVER, betray, reveal; display.

DISFAVOUR, disfigure.

DISPARAGEMENT, legal term applied to the unfitness in any way of a marriage arranged for in the case of wards.

DISPENSE WITH, grant dispensation for.

DISPLAY, extend.

DIS'PLE, discipline, teach by the whip.

DISPOSED, inclined to merriment.

DISPOSURE, disposal.

DISPRISE, depreciate.

DISPUNCT, not punctilious.

DISQUISITION, search.

DISSOLVED, enervated by grief.

DISTANCE, (?) proper measure.

DISTASTE, offence, cause of offence.

DISTASTE, render distasteful.

DISTEMPERED, upset, out of humour.

DIVISION (mus.), variation, modulation.

DOG-BOLT, term of contempt.

DOLE, given in dole, charity.

DOLE OF FACES, distribution of grimaces.

DOOM, verdict, sentence.

DOP, dip, low bow.

DOR, beetle, buzzing insect, drone, idler.

DOR, (?) buzz; "give the—," make a fool of.

DOSSER, pannier, basket.

DOTES, endowments, qualities.

DOTTEREL, plover; gull, fool.

DOUBLE, behave deceitfully.

DOXY, wench, mistress.

DRACHM, Greek silver coin.

DRESS, groom, curry.

DRESSING, coiffure.

DRIFT, intention.

DRYFOOT, track by mere scent of foot.

DUCKING, punishment for minor offences.

DUILL, grieve.

DUMPS, melancholy, originally a mournful melody.

DURINDANA, Orlando's sword.

DWINDLE, shrink away, be overawed.

EAN, yean, bring forth young.

EASINESS, readiness.

EBOLITION, ebullition.

EDGE, sword.

EECH, eke.

EGREGIOUS, eminently excellent.

EKE, also, moreover.

E-LA, highest note in the scale.

EGGS ON THE SPIT, important business on hand.

ELF-LOCK, tangled hair, supposed to be the work of elves.

EMMET, ant.

ENGAGE, involve.

ENGHLE. See Ingle.

ENGHLE, cajole; fondle.

ENGIN(E), device, contrivance; agent; ingenuity, wit.

ENGINER, engineer, deviser, plotter.

ENGINOUS, crafty, full of devices; witty, ingenious.

ENGROSS, monopolise.

ENS, an existing thing, a substance.

ENSIGNS, tokens, wounds.

ENSURE, assure.

ENTERTAIN, take into service.

ENTREAT, plead.

ENTREATY, entertainment.

ENTRY, place where a deer has lately passed.

ENVOY, denouement, conclusion.

ENVY, spite, calumny, dislike, odium.

EPHEMERIDES, calendars.

EQUAL, just, impartial.

ERECTION, elevation in esteem.

ERINGO, candied root of the sea-holly, formerly used as a sweetmeat and aphrodisiac.

ERRANT, arrant.

ESSENTIATE, become assimilated.

ESTIMATION, esteem.

ESTRICH, ostrich.

ETHNIC, heathen.

EURIPUS, flux and reflux.

EVEN, just equable.

EVENT, fate, issue.

EVENT(ED), issue(d).

EVERT, overturn.

EXACUATE, sharpen.

EXAMPLESS, without example or parallel.

EXCALIBUR, King Arthur's sword.

EXEMPLIFY, make an example of.

EXEMPT, separate, exclude.

EXEQUIES, obsequies.

EXHALE, drag out.

EXHIBITION, allowance for keep, pocket-money.

EXORBITANT, exceeding limits of propriety or law, inordinate.

EXORNATION, ornament.

EXPECT, wait.

EXPIATE, terminate.

EXPLICATE, explain, unfold.

EXTEMPORAL, extempore, unpremeditated.

EXTRACTION, essence.

EXTRAORDINARY, employed for a special or temporary purpose.

EXTRUDE, expel.

EYE, "in—," in view.

EYEBRIGHT, (?) a malt liquor in which the herb of this name was infused, or a person who sold the same (Gifford).

EYE-TINGE, least shade or gleam.

FACE, appearance.

FACES ABOUT, military word of command.

FACINOROUS, extremely wicked.

FACKINGS, faith.

FACT, deed, act, crime.

FACTIOUS, seditious, belonging to a party, given to party feeling.

FAECES, dregs.

FAGIOLI, French beans.

FAIN, forced, necessitated.

FAITHFUL, believing.

FALL, ruff or band turned back on the shoulders; or, veil.

FALSIFY, feign (fencing term).

FAME, report.

FAMILIAR, attendant spirit.

FANTASTICAL, capricious, whimsical.

FARCE, stuff.

FAR-FET. See Fet.

FARTHINGAL, hooped petticoat.

FAUCET, tapster.

FAULT, lack; loss, break in line of scent; "for—," in default of.

FAUTOR, partisan.

FAYLES, old table game similar to backgammon.

FEAR(ED), affright(ed).

FEAT, activity, operation; deed, action.

FEAT, elegant, trim.

FEE, "in—" by feudal obligation.

FEIZE, beat, belabour.

FELLOW, term of contempt.

FENNEL, emblem of flattery.

FERE, companion, fellow.

FERN-SEED, supposed to have power of rendering invisible.

FET, fetched.

FETCH, trick.

FEUTERER (Fr. vautrier), dog-keeper.

FEWMETS, dung.

FICO, fig.

FIGGUM, (?) jugglery.

FIGMENT, fiction, invention.

FIRK, frisk, move suddenly, or in jerks; "—up," stir up, rouse; "firks mad," suddenly behaves like a madman.

FIT, pay one out, punish.

FITNESS, readiness.

FITTON (FITTEN), lie, invention.

FIVE-AND-FIFTY, "highest number to stand on at primero" (Gifford).

FLAG, to fly low and waveringly.

FLAGON CHAIN, for hanging a smelling-bottle (Fr. flacon) round the neck (?). (See N.E.D.).

FLAP-DRAGON, game similar to snap-dragon.

FLASKET, some kind of basket.

FLAW, sudden gust or squall of wind.

FLAWN, custard.

FLEA, catch fleas.

FLEER, sneer, laugh derisively.

FLESH, feed a hawk or dog with flesh to incite it to the chase; initiate in blood-shed; satiate.

FLICKER-MOUSE, bat.

FLIGHT, light arrow.

FLITTER-MOUSE, bat.

FLOUT, mock, speak and act contemptuously.

FLOWERS, pulverised substance.

FLY, familiar spirit.

FOIL, weapon used in fencing; that which sets anything off to advantage.

FOIST, cut-purse, sharper.

FOND(LY), foolish(ly).

FOOT-CLOTH, housings of ornamental cloth which hung down on either side a horse to the ground.

FOOTING, foothold; footstep; dancing.

FOPPERY, foolery.

FOR, "—failing," for fear of failing.

FORBEAR, bear with; abstain from.

FORCE, "hunt at—," run the game down with dogs.

FOREHEAD, modesty; face, assurance, effrontery.

FORESLOW, delay.

FORESPEAK, bewitch; foretell.

FORETOP, front lock of hair which fashion required to be worn upright.

FORGED, fabricated.

FORM, state formally.

FORMAL, shapely; normal; conventional.

FORTHCOMING, produced when required.

FOUNDER, disable with over-riding.

FOURM, form, lair.

FOX, sword.

FRAIL, rush basket in which figs or raisins were packed.

FRAMPULL, peevish, sour-tempered.

FRAPLER, blusterer, wrangler.

FRAYING, "a stag is said to fray his head when he rubs it against a tree to... cause the outward coat of the new horns to fall off" (Gifford).

FREIGHT (of the gazetti), burden (of the newspapers).

FREQUENT, full.

FRICACE, rubbing.

FRICATRICE, woman of low character.

FRIPPERY, old clothes shop.

FROCK, smock-frock.

FROLICS, (?) humorous verses circulated at a feast (N.E.D.); couplets wrapped round sweetmeats (Cunningham).

FRONTLESS, shameless.

FROTED, rubbed.

FRUMETY, hulled wheat boiled in milk and spiced.

FRUMP, flout, sneer.

FUCUS, dye.

FUGEAND, (?) figent: fidgety, restless (N.E.D.).

FULLAM, false dice.

FULMART, polecat.

FULSOME, foul, offensive.

FURIBUND, raging, furious.

GALLEY-FOIST, city-barge, used on Lord Mayor's Day, when he was sworn into his office at Westminster (Whalley).

GALLIARD, lively dance in triple time.

GAPE, be eager after.

GARAGANTUA, Rabelais' giant.

GARB, sheaf (Fr. gerbe); manner, fashion, behaviour.

GARD, guard, trimming, gold or silver lace, or other ornament.

GARDED, faced or trimmed.

GARNISH, fee.

GAVEL-KIND, name of a land-tenure existing chiefly in Kent; from 16th century often used to denote custom of dividing a deceased man's property equally among his sons (N.E.D.).

GAZETTE, small Venetian coin worth about three-farthings.

GEANCE, jaunt, errand.

GEAR (GEER), stuff, matter, affair.

GELID, frozen.

GEMONIES, steps from which the bodies of criminals were thrown into the river.

GENERAL, free, affable.

GENIUS, attendant spirit.

GENTRY, gentlemen; manners characteristic of gentry, good breeding.

GIB-CAT, tom-cat.

GIGANTOMACHIZE, start a giants' war.

GIGLOT, wanton.

GIMBLET, gimlet.

GING, gang.

GLASS ("taking in of shadows, etc."), crystal or beryl.

GLEEK, card game played by three; party of three, trio; side glance.

GLICK (GLEEK), jest, gibe.

GLIDDER, glaze.

GLORIOUSLY, of vain glory.

GODWIT, bird of the snipe family.

GOLD-END-MAN, a buyer of broken gold and silver.

GOLL, hand.

GONFALIONIER, standard-bearer, chief magistrate, etc.

GOOD, sound in credit.

GOOD-YEAR, good luck.

GOOSE-TURD, colour of. (See Turd).

GORCROW, carrion crow.

GORGET, neck armour.

GOSSIP, godfather.

GOWKED, from "gowk," to stand staring and gaping like a fool.

GRANNAM, grandam.

GRASS, (?) grease, fat.

GRATEFUL, agreeable, welcome.

GRATIFY, give thanks to.

GRATITUDE, gratuity.

GRATULATE, welcome, congratulate.

GRAVITY, dignity.

GRAY, badger.

GRICE, cub.

GRIEF, grievance.

GRIPE, vulture, griffin.

GRIPE'S EGG, vessel in shape of.

GROAT, fourpence.

GROGRAN, coarse stuff made of silk and mohair, or of coarse silk.

GROOM-PORTER, officer in the royal household.

GROPE, handle, probe.

GROUND, pit (hence "grounded judgments").

GUARD, caution, heed.

GUARDANT, heraldic term: turning the head only.

GUILDER, Dutch coin worth about 4d.

GULES, gullet, throat; heraldic term for red.

GULL, simpleton, dupe.

GUST, taste.

HAB NAB, by, on, chance.

HABERGEON, coat of mail.

HAGGARD, wild female hawk; hence coy, wild.

HALBERD, combination of lance and battle-axe.

HALL, "a—!" a cry to clear the room for the dancers.

HANDSEL, first money taken.

HANGER, loop or strap on a sword-belt from which the sword was suspended.

HAP, fortune, luck.

HAPPILY, haply.

HAPPINESS, appropriateness, fitness.

HAPPY, rich.

HARBOUR, track, trace (an animal) to its shelter.

HARD-FAVOURED, harsh-featured.

HARPOCRATES, Horus the child, son of Osiris, figured with a finger pointing to his mouth, indicative of silence.

HARRINGTON, a patent was granted to Lord H. for the coinage of tokens (q.v.).

HARROT, herald.

HARRY NICHOLAS, founder of a community called the "Family of Love."

HAY, net for catching rabbits, etc.

HAY! (Ital. hai!), you have it (a fencing term).

HAY IN HIS HORN, ill-tempered person.

HAZARD, game at dice; that which is staked.

HEAD, "first—," young deer with antlers first sprouting; fig. a newly-ennobled man.

HEADBOROUGH, constable.

HEARKEN AFTER, inquire; "hearken out," find, search out.

HEARTEN, encourage.

HEAVEN AND HELL ("Alchemist"), names of taverns.

HECTIC, fever.

HEDGE IN, include.

HELM, upper part of a retort.

HER'NSEW, hernshaw, heron.

HIERONIMO (JERONIMO), hero of Kyd's "Spanish Tragedy."

HOBBY, nag.

HOBBY-HORSE, imitation horse of some light material, fastened round the waist of the morrice-dancer, who imitated the movements of a skittish horse.

HODDY-DODDY, fool.

HOIDEN, hoyden, formerly applied to both sexes (ancient term for leveret? Gifford).

HOLLAND, name of two famous chemists.

HONE AND HONERO, wailing expressions of lament or discontent.

HOOD-WINK'D, blindfolded.

HORARY, hourly.

HORN-MAD, stark mad (quibble).

HORN-THUMB, cut-purses were in the habit of wearing a horn shield on the thumb.

HORSE-BREAD-EATING, horses were often fed on coarse bread.

HORSE-COURSER, horse-dealer.

HOSPITAL, Christ's Hospital.

HOWLEGLAS, Eulenspiegel, the hero of a popular German tale which relates his buffooneries and knavish tricks.

HUFF, hectoring, arrogance.

HUFF IT, swagger.

HUISHER (Fr. huissier), usher.

HUM, beer and spirits mixed together.

HUMANITIAN, humanist, scholar.

HUMOROUS, capricious, moody, out of humour; moist.

HUMOUR, a word used in and out of season in the time of Shakespeare and Ben Jonson, and ridiculed by both.

HUMOURS, manners.

HUMPHREY, DUKE, those who were dinnerless spent the dinner-hour in a part of St. Paul's where stood a monument said to be that of the duke's; hence "dine with Duke Humphrey," to go hungry.

HURTLESS, harmless.

IDLE, useless, unprofitable.

ILL-AFFECTED, ill-disposed.

ILL-HABITED, unhealthy.

ILLUSTRATE, illuminate.

IMBIBITION, saturation, steeping.

IMBROCATA, fencing term: a thrust in tierce.

IMPAIR, impairment.

IMPART, give money.

IMPARTER, any one ready to be cheated and to part with his money.

IMPEACH, damage.

IMPERTINENCIES, irrelevancies.

IMPERTINENT(LY), irrelevant(ly), without reason or purpose.

IMPOSITION, duty imposed by.

IMPOTENTLY, beyond power of control.

IMPRESS, money in advance.

IMPULSION, incitement.

IN AND IN, a game played by two or three persons with four dice.

INCENSE, incite, stir up.

INCERATION, act of covering with wax; or reducing a substance to softness of wax.

INCH, "to their—es," according to their stature, capabilities.

INCH-PIN, sweet-bread.

INCONVENIENCE, inconsistency, absurdity.

INCONY, delicate, rare (used as a term of affection).

INCUBEE, incubus.

INCUBUS, evil spirit that oppresses us in sleep, nightmare.

INCURIOUS, unfastidious, uncritical.

INDENT, enter into engagement.

INDIFFERENT, tolerable, passable.

INDIGESTED, shapeless, chaotic.

INDUCE, introduce.

INDUE, supply.

INEXORABLE, relentless.

INFANTED, born, produced.

INFLAME, augment charge.

INGENIOUS, used indiscriminantly for ingenuous; intelligent, talented.

INGENUITY, ingenuousness.

INGENUOUS, generous.

INGINE. See Engin.

INGINER, engineer. (See Enginer).

INGLE, OR ENGHLE, bosom friend, intimate, minion.

INHABITABLE, uninhabitable.

INJURY, insult, affront.

IN-MATE, resident, indwelling.

INNATE, natural.

INNOCENT, simpleton.

INQUEST, jury, or other official body of inquiry.

INQUISITION, inquiry.

INSTANT, immediate.

INSTRUMENT, legal document.

INSURE, assure.

INTEGRATE, complete, perfect.

INTELLIGENCE, secret information, news.

INTEND, note carefully, attend, give ear to, be occupied with.

INTENDMENT, intention.

INTENT, intention, wish.

INTENTION, concentration of attention or gaze.

INTENTIVE, attentive.

INTERESSED, implicated.

INTRUDE, bring in forcibly or without leave.

INVINCIBLY, invisibly.

INWARD, intimate.

IRPE (uncertain), "a fantastic grimace, or contortion of the body: (Gifford)."

JACK, Jack o' the clock, automaton figure that strikes the hour; Jack-a-lent, puppet thrown at in Lent.

JACK, key of a virginal.

JACOB'S STAFF, an instrument for taking altitudes and distances.

JADE, befool.

JEALOUSY, JEALOUS, suspicion, suspicious.

JERKING, lashing.

JEW'S TRUMP, Jew's harp.

JIG, merry ballad or tune; a fanciful dialogue or light comic act introduced at the end or during an interlude of a play.

JOINED (JOINT)-STOOL, folding stool.

JOLL, jowl.

JOLTHEAD, blockhead.

JUMP, agree, tally.

JUST YEAR, no one was capable of the consulship until he was forty-three.

KELL, cocoon.

KELLY, an alchemist.

KEMB, comb.

KEMIA, vessel for distillation.

KIBE, chap, sore.

KILDERKIN, small barrel.

KILL, kiln.

KIND, nature; species; "do one's—," act according to one's nature.

KIRTLE, woman's gown of jacket and petticoat.

KISS OR DRINK AFORE ME, "this is a familiar expression, employed when what the speaker is just about to say is anticipated by another" (Gifford).

KIT, fiddle.

KNACK, snap, click.

KNIPPER-DOLING, a well-known Anabaptist.

KNITTING CUP, marriage cup.

KNOCKING, striking, weighty.

KNOT, company, band; a sandpiper or robin snipe (Tringa canutus); flower-bed laid out in fanciful design.

KURSINED, KYRSIN, christened.

LABOURED, wrought with labour and care.

LADE, load(ed).

LADING, load.

LAID, plotted.

LANCE-KNIGHT (Lanzknecht), a German mercenary foot-soldier.

LAP, fold.

LAR, household god.

LARD, garnish.

LARGE, abundant.

LARUM, alarum, call to arms.

LATTICE, tavern windows were furnished with lattices of various colours.

LAUNDER, to wash gold in aqua regia, so as imperceptibly to extract some of it.

LAVE, ladle, bale.

LAW, "give—," give a start (term of chase).

LAXATIVE, loose.

LAY ABOARD, run alongside generally with intent to board.

LEAGUER, siege, or camp of besieging army.

LEASING, lying.

LEAVE, leave off, desist.

LEER, leering or "empty, hence, perhaps, leer horse, a horse without a rider; leer is an adjective meaning uncontrolled, hence 'leer drunkards'" (Halliwell); according to Nares, a leer (empty) horse meant also a led horse; leeward, left.

LEESE, lose.

LEGS, "make—," do obeisance.

LEIGER, resident representative.

LEIGERITY, legerdemain.

LEMMA, subject proposed, or title of the epigram.

LENTER, slower.

LET, hinder.

LET, hindrance.

LEVEL COIL, a rough game... in which one hunted another from his seat. Hence used for any noisy riot (Halliwell).

LEWD, ignorant.

LEYSTALLS, receptacles of filth.

LIBERAL, ample.

LIEGER, ledger, register.

LIFT(ING), steal(ing); theft.

LIGHT, alight.

LIGHTLY, commonly, usually, often.

LIKE, please.

LIKELY, agreeable, pleasing.

LIME-HOUND, leash-, blood-hound.

LIMMER, vile, worthless.

LIN, leave off.

Line, "by—," by rule.

LINSTOCK, staff to stick in the ground, with forked head to hold a lighted match for firing cannon.

LIQUID, clear.

LIST, listen, hark; like, please.

LIVERY, legal term, delivery of the possession, etc.

LOGGET, small log, stick.

LOOSE, solution; upshot, issue; release of an arrow.

LOSE, give over, desist from; waste.

LOUTING, bowing, cringing.

LUCULENT, bright of beauty.

LUDGATHIANS, dealers on Ludgate Hill.

LURCH, rob, cheat.

LUTE, to close a vessel with some kind of cement.

MACK, unmeaning expletive.

MADGE-HOWLET or OWL, barn-owl.

MAIM, hurt, injury.

MAIN, chief concern (used as a quibble on heraldic term for "hand").

MAINPRISE, becoming surety for a prisoner so as to procure his release.

MAINTENANCE, giving aid, or abetting.

MAKE, mate.

MAKE, MADE, acquaint with business, prepare(d), instruct(ed).

MALLANDERS, disease of horses.

MALT HORSE, dray horse.

MAMMET, puppet.

MAMMOTHREPT, spoiled child.

MANAGE, control (term used for breaking-in horses); handling, administration.

MANGO, slave-dealer.

MANGONISE, polish up for sale.

MANIPLES, bundles, handfuls.

MANKIND, masculine, like a virago.

MANKIND, humanity.

MAPLE FACE, spotted face (N.E.D.).

MARCHPANE, a confection of almonds, sugar, etc.

MARK, "fly to the—," "generally said of a goshawk when, having 'put in' a covey of partridges, she takes stand, marking the spot where they disappeared from view until the falconer arrives to put them out to her" (Harting, Bibl. Accip. Gloss. 226).

MARLE, marvel.

MARROW-BONE MAN, one often on his knees for prayer.

MARRY! exclamation derived from the Virgin's name.

MARRY GIP, "probably originated from By Mary Gipcy" = St. Mary of Egypt, (N.E.D.).

MARTAGAN, Turk's cap lily.

MARYHINCHCO, stringhalt.

MASORETH, Masora, correct form of the scriptural text according to Hebrew tradition.

MASS, abb. for master.

MAUND, beg.

MAUTHER, girl, maid.

MEAN, moderation.

MEASURE, dance, more especially a stately one.

MEAT, "carry—in one's mouth," be a source of money or entertainment.

MEATH, metheglin.

MECHANICAL, belonging to mechanics, mean, vulgar.

MEDITERRANEO, middle aisle of St. Paul's, a general resort for business and amusement.

MEET WITH, even with.

MELICOTTON, a late kind of peach.

MENSTRUE, solvent.

MERCAT, market.

MERD, excrement.

MERE, undiluted; absolute, unmitigated.

MESS, party of four.

METHEGLIN, fermented liquor, of which one ingredient was honey.

METOPOSCOPY, study of physiognomy.

MIDDLING GOSSIP, go-between.

MIGNIARD, dainty, delicate.

MILE-END, training-ground of the city.

MINE-MEN, sappers.

MINION, form of cannon.

MINSITIVE, (?) mincing, affected (N.E.D.).

MISCELLANY MADAM, "a female trader in miscellaneous articles; a dealer in trinkets or ornaments of various kinds, such as kept shops in the New Exchange" (Nares).

MISCELLINE, mixed grain; medley.

MISCONCEIT, misconception.

MISPRISE, MISPRISION, mistake, misunderstanding.

MISTAKE AWAY, carry away as if by mistake.

MITHRIDATE, an antidote against poison.

MOCCINIGO, small Venetian coin, worth about ninepence.

MODERN, in the mode; ordinary, commonplace.

MOMENT, force or influence of value.

MONTANTO, upward stroke.

MONTH'S MIND, violent desire.

MOORISH, like a moor or waste.

MORGLAY, sword of Bevis of Southampton.

MORRICE-DANCE, dance on May Day, etc., in which certain personages were represented.

MORTALITY, death.

MORT-MAL, old sore, gangrene.

MOSCADINO, confection flavoured with musk.

MOTHER, Hysterica passio.

MOTION, proposal, request; puppet, puppet-show; "one of the small figures on the face of a large clock which was moved by the vibration of the pendulum" (Whalley).

MOTION, suggest, propose.

MOTLEY, parti-coloured dress of a fool; hence used to signify pertaining to, or like, a fool.

MOTTE, motto.

MOURNIVAL, set of four aces or court cards in a hand; a quartette.

MOW, setord hay or sheaves of grain.

MUCH! expressive of irony and incredulity.

MUCKINDER, handkerchief.

MULE, "born to ride on—," judges or serjeants-at-law formerly rode on mules when going in state to Westminster (Whally).

MULLETS, small pincers.

MUM-CHANCE, game of chance, played in silence.

MUN, must.

MUREY, dark crimson red.

MUSCOVY-GLASS, mica.

MUSE, wonder.

MUSICAL, in harmony.

MUSS, mouse; scramble.

MYROBOLANE, foreign conserve, "a dried plum, brought from the Indies."

MYSTERY, art, trade, profession.

NAIL, "to the—" (ad unguem), to perfection, to the very utmost.

NATIVE, natural.

NEAT, cattle.

NEAT, smartly apparelled; unmixed; dainty.

NEATLY, neatly finished.

NEATNESS, elegance.

NEIS, nose, scent.

NEUF (NEAF, NEIF), fist.

NEUFT, newt.

NIAISE, foolish, inexperienced person.

NICE, fastidious, trivial, finical, scrupulous.

NICENESS, fastidiousness.

NICK, exact amount; right moment; "set in the—," meaning uncertain.

NICE, suit, fit; hit, seize the right moment, etc., exactly hit on, hit off.

NOBLE, gold coin worth 6s. 8d.

NOCENT, harmful.

NIL, not will.

NOISE, company of musicians.

NOMENTACK, an Indian chief from Virginia.

NONES, nonce.

NOTABLE, egregious.

NOTE, sign, token.

NOUGHT, "be—," go to the devil, be hanged, etc.

NOWT-HEAD, blockhead.

NUMBER, rhythm.

NUPSON, oaf, simpleton.

OADE, woad.

OBARNI, preparation of mead.

OBJECT, oppose; expose; interpose.

OBLATRANT, barking, railing.

OBNOXIOUS, liable, exposed; offensive.

OBSERVANCE, homage, devoted service.

OBSERVANT, attentive, obsequious.

OBSERVE, show deference, respect.

OBSERVER, one who shows deference, or waits upon another.

OBSTANCY, legal phrase, "juridical opposition."

OBSTREPEROUS, clamorous, vociferous

OBSTUPEFACT, stupefied.

ODLING, (?) "must have some relation to tricking and cheating" (Nares).

OMINOUS, deadly, fatal.

ONCE, at once; for good and all; used also for additional emphasis.

ONLY, pre-eminent, special.

OPEN, make public; expound.

OPPILATION, obstruction.

OPPONE, oppose.

OPPOSITE, antagonist.

OPPRESS, suppress.

ORIGINOUS, native.

ORT, remnant, scrap.

OUT, "to be—," to have forgotten one's part; not at one with each other.

OUTCRY, sale by auction.

OUTRECUIDANCE, arrogance, presumption.

OUTSPEAK, speak more than.

OVERPARTED, given too difficult a part to play.

OWLSPIEGEL. See Howleglass.

OYEZ! (O YES!), hear ye! call of the public crier when about to make a proclamation.

PACKING PENNY, "give a—," dismiss, send packing.

PAD, highway.

PAD-HORSE, road-horse.

PAINED (PANED) SLOPS, full breeches made of strips of different colour and material.

PAINFUL, diligent, painstaking.

PAINT, blush.

PALINODE, ode of recantation.

PALL, weaken, dim, make stale.

PALM, triumph.

PAN, skirt of dress or coat.

PANNEL, pad, or rough kind of saddle.

PANNIER-ALLY, inhabited by tripe-sellers.

PANNIER-MAN, hawker; a man employed about the inns of court to bring in provisions, set the table, etc.

PANTOFLE, indoor shoe, slipper.

PARAMENTOS, fine trappings.

PARANOMASIE, a play upon words.

PARANTORY, (?) peremptory.

PARCEL, particle, fragment (used contemptuously); article.

PARCEL, part, partly.

PARCEL-POET, poetaster.

PARERGA, subordinate matters.

PARGET, to paint or plaster the face.

PARLE, parley.

PARLOUS, clever, shrewd.

PART, apportion.

PARTAKE, participate in.

PARTED, endowed, talented.

PARTICULAR, individual person.

PARTIZAN, kind of halberd.

PARTRICH, partridge.

PARTS, qualities, endowments.

PASH, dash, smash.

PASS, care, trouble oneself.

PASSADO, fencing term: a thrust.

PASSAGE, game at dice.

PASSINGLY, exceedingly.

PASSION, effect caused by external agency.

PASSION, "in—," in so melancholy a tone, so pathetically.

PATOUN, (?) Fr. Paton, pellet of dough; perhaps the "moulding of the tobacco... for the pipe" (Gifford); (?) variant of Petun, South American name of tobacco.

PATRICO, the recorder, priest, orator of strolling beggars or gipsies.

PATTEN, shoe with wooden sole; "go—," keep step with, accompany.

PAUCA VERBA, few words.

PAVIN, a stately dance.

PEACE, "with my master's—," by leave, favour.

PECULIAR, individual, single.

PEDANT, teacher of the languages.

PEEL, baker's shovel.

PEEP, speak in a small or shrill voice.

PEEVISH(LY), foolish(ly), capricious(ly); childish(ly).

PELICAN, a retort fitted with tube or tubes, for continuous distillation.

PENCIL, small tuft of hair.

PERDUE, soldier accustomed to hazardous service.

PEREMPTORY, resolute, bold; imperious; thorough, utter, absolute(ly).

PERIMETER, circumference of a figure.

PERIOD, limit, end.

PERK, perk up.

PERPETUANA, "this seems to be that glossy kind of stuff now called everlasting, and anciently worn by serjeants and other city officers" (Gifford).

PERSPECTIVE, a view, scene or scenery; an optical device which gave a distortion to the picture unless seen from a particular point; a relief, modelled to produce an optical illusion.

PERSPICIL, optic glass.

PERSTRINGE, criticise, censure.

PERSUADE, inculcate, commend.

PERSWAY, mitigate.

PERTINACY, pertinacity.

PESTLING, pounding, pulverising, like a pestle.

PETASUS, broad-brimmed hat or winged cap worn by Mercury.

PETITIONARY, supplicatory.

PETRONEL, a kind of carbine or light gun carried by horsemen.

PETULANT, pert, insolent.

PHERE. See Fere.

PHLEGMA, watery distilled liquor (old chem. "water").

PHRENETIC, madman.

PICARDIL, stiff upright collar fastened on to the coat (Whalley).

PICT-HATCH, disreputable quarter of London.

PIECE, person, used for woman or girl; a gold coin worth in Jonson's time 20s. or 22s.

PIECES OF EIGHT, Spanish coin: piastre equal to eight reals.

PIED, variegated.

PIE-POUDRES (Fr. pied-poudreux, dusty-foot), court held at fairs to administer justice to itinerant vendors and buyers.

PILCHER, term of contempt; one who wore a buff or leather jerkin, as did the serjeants of the counter; a pilferer.

PILED, pilled, peeled, bald.

PILL'D, polled, fleeced.

PIMLICO, "sometimes spoken of as a person—perhaps master of a house famous for a particular ale" (Gifford).

PINE, afflict, distress.

PINK, stab with a weapon; pierce or cut in scallops for ornament.

PINNACE, a go-between in infamous sense.

PISMIRE, ant.

PISTOLET, gold coin, worth about 6s.

PITCH, height of a bird of prey's flight.

PLAGUE, punishment, torment.

PLAIN, lament.

PLAIN SONG, simple melody.

PLAISE, plaice.

PLANET, "struck with a—," planets were supposed to have powers of blasting or exercising secret influences.

PLAUSIBLE, pleasing.

PLAUSIBLY, approvingly.

PLOT, plan.

PLY, apply oneself to.

POESIE, posy, motto inside a ring.

POINT IN HIS DEVICE, exact in every particular.

POINTS, tagged laces or cords for fastening the breeches to the doublet.

POINT-TRUSSER, one who trussed (tied) his master's points (q.v.).

POISE, weigh, balance.

POKING-STICK, stick used for setting the plaits of ruffs.

POLITIC, politician.

POLITIC, judicious, prudent, political.

POLITICIAN, plotter, intriguer.

POLL, strip, plunder, gain by extortion.

POMANDER, ball of perfume, worn or hung about the person to prevent infection, or for foppery.

POMMADO, vaulting on a horse without the aid of stirrups.

PONTIC, sour.

POPULAR, vulgar, of the populace.

POPULOUS, numerous.

PORT, gate; print of a deer's foot.

PORT, transport.

PORTAGUE, Portuguese gold coin, worth over 3 or 4 pounds.

PORTCULLIS, "—of coin," some old coins have a portcullis stamped on their reverse (Whalley).

PORTENT, marvel, prodigy; sinister omen.

PORTENTOUS, prophesying evil, threatening.

PORTER, references appear "to allude to Parsons, the king's porter, who was... near seven feet high" (Whalley).

POSSESS, inform, acquaint.

POST AND PAIR, a game at cards.

POSY, motto. (See Poesie).

POTCH, poach.

POULT-FOOT, club-foot.

POUNCE, claw, talon.

PRACTICE, intrigue, concerted plot.

PRACTISE, plot, conspire.

PRAGMATIC, an expert, agent.

PRAGMATIC, officious, conceited, meddling.

PRECEDENT, record of proceedings.

PRECEPT, warrant, summons.

PRECISIAN(ISM), Puritan(ism), preciseness.

PREFER, recommend.

PRESENCE, presence chamber.

PRESENT(LY), immediate(ly), without delay; at the present time; actually.

PRESS, force into service.

PREST, ready.

PRETEND, assert, allege.

PREVENT, anticipate.

PRICE, worth, excellence.

PRICK, point, dot used in the writing of Hebrew and other languages.

PRICK, prick out, mark off, select; trace, track; "—away," make off with speed.

PRIMERO, game of cards.

PRINCOX, pert boy.

PRINT, "in—," to the letter, exactly.

PRISTINATE, former.

PRIVATE, private interests.

PRIVATE, privy, intimate.

PROCLIVE, prone to.

PRODIGIOUS, monstrous, unnatural.

PRODIGY, monster.

PRODUCED, prolonged.

PROFESS, pretend.

PROJECTION, the throwing of the "powder of projection" into the crucible to turn the melted metal into gold or silver.

PROLATE, pronounce drawlingly.

PROPER, of good appearance, handsome; own, particular.

PROPERTIES, stage necessaries.

PROPERTY, duty; tool.

PRORUMPED, burst out.

PROTEST, vow, proclaim (an affected word of that time); formally declare non-payment, etc., of bill of exchange; fig. failure of personal credit, etc.

PROVANT, soldier's allowance—hence, of common make.

PROVIDE, foresee.

PROVIDENCE, foresight, prudence.

PUBLICATION, making a thing public of common property (N.E.D.).

PUCKFIST, puff-ball; insipid, insignificant, boasting fellow.

PUFF-WING, shoulder puff.

PUISNE, judge of inferior rank, a junior.

PULCHRITUDE, beauty.

PUMP, shoe.

PUNGENT, piercing.

PUNTO, point, hit.

PURCEPT, precept, warrant.

PURE, fine, capital, excellent.

PURELY, perfectly, utterly.

PURL, pleat or fold of a ruff.

PURSE-NET, net of which the mouth is drawn together with a string.

PURSUIVANT, state messenger who summoned the persecuted seminaries; warrant officer.

PURSY, PURSINESS, shortwinded(ness).

PUT, make a push, exert yourself (N.E.D.).

PUT OFF, excuse, shift.

PUT ON, incite, encourage; proceed with, take in hand, try.

QUACKSALVER, quack.

QUAINT, elegant, elaborated, ingenious, clever.

QUAR, quarry.

QUARRIED, seized, or fed upon, as prey.

QUEAN, hussy, jade.

QUEASY, hazardous, delicate.

QUELL, kill, destroy.

QUEST, request; inquiry.

QUESTION, decision by force of arms.

QUESTMAN, one appointed to make official inquiry.

QUIB, QUIBLIN, quibble, quip.

QUICK, the living.

QUIDDIT, quiddity, legal subtlety.

QUIRK, clever turn or trick.

QUIT, requite, repay; acquit, absolve; rid; forsake, leave.

QUITTER-BONE, disease of horses.

QUODLING, codling.

QUOIT, throw like a quoit, chuck.

QUOTE, take note, observe, write down.

RACK, neck of mutton or pork (Halliwell).

RAKE UP, cover over.

RAMP, rear, as a lion, etc.

RAPT, carry away.

RAPT, enraptured.

RASCAL, young or inferior deer.

RASH, strike with a glancing oblique blow, as a boar with its tusk.

RATSEY, GOMALIEL, a famous highwayman.

RAVEN, devour.

REACH, understand.

REAL, regal.

REBATU, ruff, turned-down collar.

RECTOR, RECTRESS, director, governor.

REDARGUE, confute.

REDUCE, bring back.

REED, rede, counsel, advice.

REEL, run riot.

REFEL, refute.

REFORMADOES, disgraced or disbanded soldiers.

REGIMENT, government.

REGRESSION, return.

REGULAR ("Tale of a Tub"), regular noun (quibble) (N.E.D.).

RELIGION, "make—of," make a point of, scruple of.

RELISH, savour.

REMNANT, scrap of quotation.

REMORA, species of fish.

RENDER, depict, exhibit, show.

REPAIR, reinstate.

REPETITION, recital, narration.

REREMOUSE, bat.

RESIANT, rorident

RESIDENCE, sediment.

RESOLUTION, judgment, decision.

RESOLVE, inform; assure; prepare, make up one's mind; dissolve; come to a decision, be convinced; relax, set at ease.

RESPECTIVE, worthy of respect; regardful, discriminative.

RESPECTIVELY, with reverence.

RESPECTLESS, regardless.

RESPIRE, exhale; inhale.

RESPONSIBLE, correspondent.

REST, musket-rest.

REST, "set up one's—," venture one's all, one's last stake (from game of primero).

REST, arrest.

RESTIVE, RESTY, dull, inactive.

RETCHLESS(NESS), reckless(ness).

RETIRE, cause to retire.

RETRICATO, fencing term.

RETRIEVE, rediscovery of game once sprung.

RETURNS, ventures sent abroad, for the safe return of which so much money is received.

REVERBERATE, dissolve or blend by reflected heat.

REVERSE, REVERSO, back-handed thrust, etc., in fencing.

REVISE, reconsider a sentence.

RHEUM, spleen, caprice.

RIBIBE, abusive term for an old woman.

RID, destroy, do away with.

RIFLING, raffling, dicing.

RING, "cracked within the—," coins so cracked were unfit for currency.

RISSE, risen, rose.

RIVELLED, wrinkled.

ROARER, swaggerer.

ROCHET, fish of the gurnet kind.

ROCK, distaff.

RODOMONTADO, braggadocio.

ROGUE, vagrant, vagabond.

RONDEL, "a round mark in the score of a public-house" (Nares); roundel.

ROOK, sharper; fool, dupe.

ROSAKER, similar to ratsbane.

ROSA-SOLIS, a spiced spirituous liquor.

ROSES, rosettes.

ROUND, "gentlemen of the—," officers of inferior rank.

ROUND TRUNKS, trunk hose, short loose breeches reaching almost or quite to the knees.

ROUSE, carouse, bumper.

ROVER, arrow used for shooting at a random mark at uncertain distance.

ROWLY-POWLY, roly-poly.

RUDE, RUDENESS, unpolished, rough(ness), coarse(ness).

RUFFLE, flaunt, swagger.

RUG, coarse frieze.

RUG-GOWNS, gown made of rug.

RUSH, reference to rushes with which the floors were then strewn.

RUSHER, one who strewed the floor with rushes.

RUSSET, homespun cloth of neutral or reddish-brown colour.

SACK, loose, flowing gown.

SADLY, seriously, with gravity,

SAD(NESS), sober, serious(ness).

SAFFI, bailiffs.

ST. THOMAS A WATERINGS, place in Surrey where criminals were executed.

SAKER, small piece of ordnance.

SALT, leap.

SALT, lascivious.

SAMPSUCHINE, sweet marjoram.

SARABAND, a slow dance.

SATURNALS, began December 17.

SAUCINESS, presumption, insolence.

SAUCY, bold, impudent, wanton.

SAUNA (Lat.), a gesture of contempt.

SAVOUR, perceive; gratify, please; to partake of the nature.

SAY, sample.

SAY, assay, try.

SCALD, word of contempt, implying dirt and disease.

SCALLION, shalot, small onion.

SCANDERBAG, "name which the Turks (in allusion to Alexander the Great) gave to the brave Castriot, chief of Albania, with whom they had continual wars. His romantic life had just been translated" (Gifford).

SCAPE, escape.

SCARAB, beetle.

SCARTOCCIO, fold of paper, cover, cartouch, cartridge.

SCONCE, head.

SCOPE, aim.

SCOT AND LOT, tax, contribution (formerly a parish assessment).

SCOTOMY, dizziness in the head.

SCOUR, purge.

SCOURSE, deal, swap.

SCRATCHES, disease of horses.

SCROYLE, mean, rascally fellow.

SCRUPLE, doubt.

SEAL, put hand to the giving up of property or rights.

SEALED, stamped as genuine.

SEAM-RENT, ragged.

SEAMING LACES, insertion or edging.

SEAR UP, close by searing, burning.

SEARCED, sifted.

SECRETARY, able to keep a secret.

SECULAR, worldly, ordinary, commonplace.

SECURE, confident.

SEELIE, happy, blest.

SEISIN, legal term: possession.

SELLARY, lewd person.

SEMBLABLY, similarly.

SEMINARY, a Romish priest educated in a foreign seminary.

SENSELESS, insensible, without sense or feeling.

SENSIBLY, perceptibly.

SENSIVE, sensitive.

SENSUAL, pertaining to the physical or material.

SERENE, harmful dew of evening.

SERICON, red tincture.

SERVANT, lover.

SERVICES, doughty deeds of arms.

SESTERCE, Roman copper coin.

SET, stake, wager.

SET UP, drill.

SETS, deep plaits of the ruff.

SEWER, officer who served up the feast, and brought water for the hands of the guests.

SHAPE, a suit by way of disguise.

SHIFT, fraud, dodge.

SHIFTER, cheat.

SHITTLE, shuttle; "shittle-cock," shuttlecock.

SHOT, tavern reckoning.

SHOT-CLOG, one only tolerated because he paid the shot (reckoning) for the rest.

SHOT-FREE, scot-free, not having to pay.

SHOVE-GROAT, low kind of gambling amusement, perhaps somewhat of the nature of pitch and toss.

SHOT-SHARKS, drawers.

SHREWD, mischievous, malicious, curst.

SHREWDLY, keenly, in a high degree.

SHRIVE, sheriff; posts were set up before his door for proclamations, or to indicate his residence.

SHROVING, Shrovetide, season of merriment.

SIGILLA, seal, mark.

SILENCED BRETHERN, MINISTERS, those of the Church or Nonconformists who had been silenced, deprived, etc.

SILLY, simple, harmless.

SIMPLE, silly, witless; plain, true.

SIMPLES, herbs.

SINGLE, term of chase, signifying when the hunted stag is separated from the herd, or forced to break covert.

SINGLE, weak, silly.

SINGLE-MONEY, small change.

SINGULAR, unique, supreme.

SI-QUIS, bill, advertisement.

SKELDRING, getting money under false pretences; swindling.

SKILL, "it—s not," matters not.

SKINK(ER), pour, draw(er), tapster.

SKIRT, tail.

SLEEK, smooth.

SLICE, fire shovel or pan (dial.).

SLICK, sleek, smooth.

'SLID, 'SLIGHT, 'SPRECIOUS, irreverent oaths.

SLIGHT, sleight, cunning, cleverness; trick.

SLIP, counterfeit coin, bastard.

SLIPPERY, polished and shining.

SLOPS, large loose breeches.

SLOT, print of a stag's foot.

SLUR, put a slur on; cheat (by sliding a die in some way).

SMELT, gull, simpleton.

SNORLE, "perhaps snarl, as Puppy is addressed" (Cunningham).

SNOTTERIE, filth.

SNUFF, anger, resentment; "take in—," take offence at.

SNUFFERS, small open silver dishes for holding snuff, or receptacle for placing snuffers in (Halliwell).

SOCK, shoe worn by comic actors.

SOD, seethe.

SOGGY, soaked, sodden.

SOIL, "take—," said of a hunted stag when he takes to the water for safety.

SOL, sou.

SOLDADOES, soldiers.

SOLICIT, rouse, excite to action.

SOOTH, flattery, cajolery.

SOOTHE, flatter, humour.

SOPHISTICATE, adulterate.

SORT, company, party; rank, degree.

SORT, suit, fit; select.

SOUSE, ear.

SOUSED ("Devil is an Ass"), fol. read "sou't," which Dyce interprets as "a variety of the spelling of "shu'd": to "shu" is to scare a bird away." (See his "Webster," page 350).

SOWTER, cobbler.

SPAGYRICA, chemistry according to the teachings of Paracelsus.

SPAR, bar.

SPEAK, make known, proclaim.

SPECULATION, power of sight.

SPED, to have fared well, prospered.

SPEECE, species.

SPIGHT, anger, rancour.

SPINNER, spider.

SPINSTRY, lewd person.

SPITTLE, hospital, lazar-house.

SPLEEN, considered the seat of the emotions.

SPLEEN, caprice, humour, mood.

SPRUNT, spruce.

SPURGE, foam.

SPUR-RYAL, gold coin worth 15s.

SQUIRE, square, measure; "by the—," exactly.

STAGGERING, wavering, hesitating.

STAIN, disparagement, disgrace.

STALE, decoy, or cover, stalking-horse.

STALE, make cheap, common.

STALK, approach stealthily or under cover.

STALL, forestall.

STANDARD, suit.

STAPLE, market, emporium.

STARK, downright.

STARTING-HOLES, loopholes of escape.

STATE, dignity; canopied chair of state; estate.

STATUMINATE, support vines by poles or stakes; used by Pliny (Gifford).

STAY, gag.

STAY, await; detain.

STICKLER, second or umpire.

STIGMATISE, mark, brand.

STILL, continual(ly), constant(ly).

STINKARD, stinking fellow.

STINT, stop.

STIPTIC, astringent,

STOCCATA, thrust in fencing.

STOCK-FISH, salted and dried fish.

STOMACH, pride, valour.

STOMACH, resent.

STOOP, swoop down as a hawk.

STOP, fill, stuff.

STOPPLE, stopper.

STOTE, stoat, weasel.

STOUP, stoop, swoop=bow.

STRAIGHT, straightway.

STRAMAZOUN (Ital. stramazzone), a down blow, as opposed to the thrust.

STRANGE, like a stranger, unfamiliar.

STRANGENESS, distance of behaviour.

STREIGHTS, OR BERMUDAS, labyrinth of alleys and courts in the Strand.

STRIGONIUM, Grau in Hungary, taken from the Turks in 1597.

STRIKE, balance (accounts).

STRINGHALT, disease of horses.

STROKER, smoother, flatterer.

STROOK, p.p. of "strike."

STRUMMEL-PATCHED, strummel is glossed in dialect dicts. as "a long, loose and dishevelled head of hair."

STUDIES, studious efforts.

STYLE, title; pointed instrument used for writing on wax tablets.

SUBTLE, fine, delicate, thin; smooth, soft.

SUBTLETY (SUBTILITY), subtle device.

SUBURB, connected with loose living.

SUCCUBAE, demons in form of women.

SUCK, extract money from.

SUFFERANCE, suffering.

SUMMED, term of falconry: with full-grown plumage.

SUPER-NEGULUM, topers turned the cup bottom up when it was empty.

SUPERSTITIOUS, over-scrupulous.

SUPPLE, to make pliant.

SURBATE, make sore with walking.

SURCEASE, cease.

SUR-REVERENCE, save your reverence.

SURVISE, peruse.

SUSCITABILITY, excitability.

SUSPECT, suspicion.

SUSPEND, suspect.

SUSPENDED, held over for the present.

SUTLER, victualler.

SWAD, clown, boor.

SWATH BANDS, swaddling clothes.

SWINGE, beat.

TABERD, emblazoned mantle or tunic worn by knights and heralds.

TABLE(S), "pair of—," tablets, note-book.

TABOR, small drum.

TABRET, labor.

TAFFETA, silk; "tuft-taffeta," a more costly silken fabric.

TAINT, "—a staff," break a lance at tilting in an unscientific or dishonourable manner.

TAKE IN, capture, subdue.

TAKE ME WITH YOU, let me understand you.

TAKE UP, obtain on credit, borrow.

TALENT, sum or weight of Greek currency.

TALL, stout, brave.

TANKARD-BEARERS, men employed to fetch water from the conduits.

TARLETON, celebrated comedian and jester.

TARTAROUS, like a Tartar.

TAVERN-TOKEN, "to swallow a—," get drunk.

TELL, count.

TELL-TROTH, truth-teller.

TEMPER, modify, soften.

TENDER, show regard, care for, cherish; manifest.

TENT, "take—," take heed.

TERSE, swept and polished.

TERTIA, "that portion of an army levied out of one particular district or division of a country" (Gifford).

TESTON, tester, coin worth 6d.

THIRDBOROUGH, constable.

THREAD, quality.

THREAVES, droves.

THREE-FARTHINGS, piece of silver current under Elizabeth.

THREE-PILED, of finest quality, exaggerated.

THRIFTILY, carefully.

THRUMS, ends of the weaver's warp; coarse yarn made from.

THUMB-RING, familiar spirits were supposed capable of being carried about in various ornaments or parts of dress.

TIBICINE, player on the tibia, or pipe.

TICK-TACK, game similar to backgammon.

TIGHTLY, promptly.

TIM, (?) expressive of a climax of nonentity.

TIMELESS, untimely, unseasonable.

TINCTURE, an essential or spiritual principle supposed by alchemists to be transfusible into material things; an imparted characteristic or tendency.

TINK, tinkle.

TIPPET, "turn—," change behaviour or way of life.

TIPSTAFF, staff tipped with metal.

TIRE, head-dress.

TIRE, feed ravenously, like a bird of prey.

TITILLATION, that which tickles the senses, as a perfume.

TOD, fox.

TOILED, worn out, harassed.

TOKEN, piece of base metal used in place of very small coin, when this was scarce.

TONNELS, nostrils.

TOP, "parish—," large top kept in villages for amusement and exercise in frosty weather when people were out of work.

TOTER, tooter, player on a wind instrument.

TOUSE, pull, rend.

TOWARD, docile, apt; on the way to; as regards; present, at hand.

TOY, whim; trick; term of contempt.

TRACT, attraction.

TRAIN, allure, entice.

TRANSITORY, transmittable.

TRANSLATE, transform.

TRAY-TRIP, game at dice (success depended on throwing a three) (Nares).

TREACHOUR (TRECHER), traitor.

TREEN, wooden.

TRENCHER, serving-man who carved or served food.

TRENDLE-TAIL, trundle-tail, curly-tailed.

TRICK (TRICKING), term of heraldry: to draw outline of coat of arms, etc., without blazoning.

TRIG, a spruce, dandified man.

TRILL, trickle.

TRILLIBUB, tripe, any worthless, trifling thing.

TRIPOLY, "come from—," able to perform feats of agility, a "jest nominal," depending on the first part of the word (Gifford).

TRITE, worn, shabby.

TRIVIA, three-faced goddess (Hecate).

TROJAN, familiar term for an equal or inferior; thief.

TROLL, sing loudly.

TROMP, trump, deceive.

TROPE, figure of speech.

TROW, think, believe, wonder.

TROWLE, troll.

TROWSES, breeches, drawers.

TRUCHMAN, interpreter.

TRUNDLE, JOHN, well-known printer.

TRUNDLE, roll, go rolling along.

TRUNDLING CHEATS, term among gipsies and beggars for carts or coaches (Gifford).

TRUNK, speaking-tube.

TRUSS, tie the tagged laces that fastened the breeches to the doublet.

TUBICINE, trumpeter.

TUCKET (Ital. toccato), introductory flourish on the trumpet.

TUITION, guardianship.

TUMBLER, a particular kind of dog so called from the mode of his hunting.

TUMBREL-SLOP, loose, baggy breeches.

TURD, excrement.

TUSK, gnash the teeth (Century Dict.).

TWIRE, peep, twinkle.

TWOPENNY ROOM, gallery.

TYRING-HOUSE, attiring-room.

ULENSPIEGEL. See Howleglass.

UMBRATILE, like or pertaining to a shadow.

UMBRE, brown dye.

UNBATED, unabated.

UNBORED, (?) excessively bored.

UNCARNATE, not fleshly, or of flesh.

UNCOUTH, strange, unusual.

UNDERTAKER, "one who undertook by his influence in the House of Commons to carry things agreeably to his Majesty's wishes" (Whalley); one who becomes surety for.

UNEQUAL, unjust.

UNEXCEPTED, no objection taken at.

UNFEARED, unaffrighted.

UNHAPPILY, unfortunately.

UNICORN'S HORN, supposed antidote to poison.

UNKIND(LY), unnatural(ly).

UNMANNED, untamed (term in falconry).

UNQUIT, undischarged.

UNREADY, undressed.

UNRUDE, rude to an extreme.

UNSEASONED, unseasonable, unripe.

UNSEELED, a hawk's eyes were "seeled" by sewing the eyelids together with fine thread.

UNTIMELY, unseasonably.

UNVALUABLE, invaluable.

UPBRAID, make a matter of reproach.

UPSEE, heavy kind of Dutch beer (Halliwell); "—Dutch," in the Dutch fashion.

UPTAILS ALL, refrain of a popular song.

URGE, allege as accomplice, instigator.

URSHIN, URCHIN, hedgehog.

USE, interest on money; part of sermon dealing with the practical application of doctrine.

USE, be in the habit of, accustomed to; put out to interest.

USQUEBAUGH, whisky.

USURE, usury.

UTTER, put in circulation, make to pass current; put forth for sale.

VAIL, bow, do homage.

VAILS, tips, gratuities.

VALL. See Vail.

VALLIES (Fr. valise), portmanteau, bag.

VAPOUR(S) (n. and v.), used affectedly, like "humour," in many senses, often very vaguely and freely ridiculed by Jonson; humour, disposition, whims, brag(ging), hector(ing), etc.

VARLET, bailiff, or serjeant-at-mace.

VAUT, vault.

VEER (naut.), pay out.

VEGETAL, vegetable; person full of life and vigour.

VELLUTE, velvet.

VELVET CUSTARD. Cf. "Taming of the Shrew," iv. 3, 82, "custard coffin," coffin being the raised crust over a pie.

VENT, vend, sell; give outlet to; scent, snuff up.

VENUE, bout (fencing term).

VERDUGO (Span.), hangman, executioner.

VERGE, "in the—," within a certain distance of the court.

VEX, agitate, torment.

VICE, the buffoon of old moralities; some kind of machinery for moving a puppet (Gifford).

VIE AND REVIE, to hazard a certain sum, and to cover it with a larger one.

VINCENT AGAINST YORK, two heralds-at-arms.

VINDICATE, avenge.

VIRGE, wand, rod.

VIRGINAL, old form of piano.

VIRTUE, valour.

VIVELY, in lifelike manner, livelily.

VIZARD, mask.

VOGUE, rumour, gossip.

VOICE, vote.

VOID, leave, quit.

VOLARY, cage, aviary.

VOLLEY, "at—," "o' the volee," at random (from a term of tennis).

VORLOFFE, furlough.

WADLOE, keeper of the Devil Tavern, where Jonson and his friends met in the 'Apollo' room (Whalley).

WAIGHTS, waits, night musicians, "band of musical watchmen" (Webster), or old form of "hautboys."

WANNION, "vengeance," "plague" (Nares).

WARD, a famous pirate.

WARD, guard in fencing.

WATCHET, pale, sky blue.

WEAL, welfare.

WEED, garment.

WEFT, waif.

WEIGHTS, "to the gold—," to every minute particular.

WELKIN, sky.

WELL-SPOKEN, of fair speech.

WELL-TORNED, turned and polished, as on a wheel.

WELT, hem, border of fur.

WHER, whether.

WHETSTONE, GEORGE, an author who lived 1544(?) to 1587(?).

WHIFF, a smoke, or drink; "taking the—," inhaling the tobacco smoke or some such accomplishment.

WHIGH-HIES, neighings, whinnyings.

WHIMSY, whim, "humour."

WHINILING, (?) whining, weakly.

WHIT, (?) a mere jot.

WHITEMEAT, food made of milk or eggs.

WICKED, bad, clumsy.

WICKER, pliant, agile.

WILDING, esp. fruit of wild apple or crab tree (Webster).

WINE, "I have the—for you," Prov.: I have the perquisites (of the office) which you are to share (Cunningham).

WINNY, "same as old word "wonne," to stay, etc." (Whalley).

WISE-WOMAN, fortune-teller.

WISH, recommend.

WISS (WUSSE), "I—," certainly, of a truth.

WITHOUT, beyond.

WITTY, cunning, ingenious, clever.

WOOD, collection, lot.

WOODCOCK, term of contempt.

WOOLSACK ("—pies"), name of tavern.

WORT, unfermented beer.

WOUNDY, great, extreme.

WREAK, revenge.

WROUGHT, wrought upon.

WUSSE, interjection. (See Wiss).

YEANLING, lamb, kid.

ZANY, an inferior clown, who attended upon the chief fool and mimicked his tricks.

www.ingramcontent.com/pod-product-compliance
Lightning Source LLC
LaVergne TN
LVHW021500080426
835509LV00018B/2350